Laura Courage, The Debtor Do̶ ̶ ̶ ̶ ̶ ̶ ̶ ̶
helping clients Get Out of Debt. ̶ ̶ ̶ ̶ ̶ ̶ ̶ ̶
& Grady, PLLC and its primary lo̶c̶a̶t̶i̶o̶n̶ ̶i̶s̶ ̶a̶t̶ ̶2̶2̶5̶ ̶G̶r̶e̶e̶n̶f̶i̶e̶l̶d̶
Parkway, Suite 107, *Liverpool*, 13088, just north of *Syracuse*,
New York in **Onondaga** County.

The firm has 10 additional branch offices to meet with clients in
>   *New Hartford* (**Oneida** County),
>   *Binghamton* (**Broome** County and serving **Tioga** County),
>   *Watertown* (**Jefferson** County and serving **St. Lawrence** and
>   **Lewis** Counties),
>   *Auburn* (**Cayuga** County),
>   *Fulton* (**Oswego** County),
>   *Homer* (**Cortland** County and serving **Tompkins** County),
>   *Oneida* (**Madison** County),
>   *Norwich* (**Chenango** County),
>   *Oneonta* (**Otsego** County and serving **Delaware** County) and
>   *Herkimer* (**Herkimer** County and serving **Montgomery** and
>   **Fulton** Counties).

The firm's primary website is www.harrisbankruptcy.com which includes a blog about getting out of debt and saving money.

You can contact Laura Courage via email at laura@ harrisbankruptcy.com

Also *Like* **The Debtor Doctor** on *FACEBOOK* and see funny cartoons regarding money or *follow* Laura on Twitter﹖ @ **TheDebtorDoctor**.

or call 1-855-CNY-ATTY (1-855-269-2889).

We are a debt relief agency. Prior results do not guarantee future results.

BEST WAY TO GET OUT OF DEBT

BEST WAY TO GET OUT OF DEBT

LAURA COURAGE
THE DEBTOR DOCTOR ™

WORD ASSOCIATION PUBLISHERS
www.wordassociation.com
1.800.827.7903

ISBN: 978-1-59571-929-4

Designed and published by
Word Association Publishers
205 Fifth Avenue
Tarentum, Pennsylvania 15084

www.wordassociation.com

1.800.827.7903

TABLE OF CONTENTS

Foreword 11

Introduction 15

The Best Ways to Get Out of Debt 19

    Bankruptcy—Chapter 7 22

    Add Upon Repayment Plan 29

Second-Best Choices 38

    Bankruptcy—Chapter 13 38

    Negotiating with Creditors 44

    Consumer Credit Counseling 49

    Reverse-Mortgage Strategy 54

    Creditor Call Relief Program Strategy 58

    Fighting Creditors 62

Options to Avoid if Possible 69

    Robbing Peter to Pay Paul—Crisis Management 69

    Gambling 73

    Debt-Reduction Strategy 77

    Borrowing from Relatives 84

    Consolidating Debt 89

    Using One Credit Card to Pay Another Credit Card ..93

    Getting a Second Mortgage 97

    Using Retirement Funds 100

    Working Multiple Jobs 104

Selling Assets 108

Payday Loans 112

Doing Nothing 113

Special Debt Situations 117

Mortgage Foreclosure/Modification Strategies 117

Tax Repayment Strategies 124

Student Loan Repayment Strategies 135

Debt-Management Strategies for Members of the
Military 145

Information for Professionals Helping Others
Get Out of Debt 150

About the Author 162

Author's Note: This book is intended for people living in Upstate New York only; some of the information contained herein will not apply to those living in Downstate New York or in other parts of the country. Harris-Courage & Grady, PLLC is a debt-relief agency. This is Attorney Advertising. The information in this book is designed for general information only. The information presented in this book should not be construed to be formal legal advice nor the formation of a lawyer/client relationship.

FOREWORD

As is the case with many Americans, my husband and I finished our educations only to find ourselves in serious debt due to student loans, credit cards, and a new car. My husband accepted a job in Upstate New York, the best job he could find, which was over 2,000 miles away from the support of family and friends. We had an infant and a four-year-old.

I drove alone to New York with our infant to search for a job and a place to live while my husband finished his final class work. For two months, my baby and I had no permanent place to live in New York, and it was quite an adventure, to say the least. Even though I would have loved to have stayed at home with my children and not work, I had to help pay off our debts.

When my husband and I finally found an apartment, heat and hot water were scarce, and the noise level was high, especially on Friday and Saturday nights. On top of that, as is the case with most people deep in debt, we were one mishap away from disaster. We were already living paycheck to paycheck. After a few months, my husband totaled his new car; we didn't have sufficient insurance, so we owed on a car we didn't have anymore. When I figured out our budget, I saw we had less disposable income than when we were in college. We had no money for fun or to visit our families, and no way to save money. I remember hiding my husband's catalogs in hopes he wouldn't spend any money, and I'm sure he was frustrated about whatever I spent money on.

It felt like we were on a treadmill to nowhere. We had no idea where to get help or what our options were. I became extremely depressed; I couldn't sleep, and I felt the crushing weight of the world on my shoulders. My husband and I fought about money, time, and resources. I was embarrassed about our situation even though we were trying to do the right thing.

Our debt situation lasted years. It would break my heart to hear my children pray at family prayer time that we would get out of debt so we, as parents, could spend more time with them. I missed our children's sporting events and concerts, and I cancelled dates with my husband to get in some overtime at work. My relationship with my husband deteriorated, and our marriage ultimately ended in divorce. My children would complain that I never spent time with them. I didn't have many friends because I had no time to spend with them and didn't want to admit I couldn't afford to go places with them. I borrowed money from my sister to consolidate our debts, and although we paid her off, she no longer wants any type of relationship with me. I was so focused on getting out of debt that I failed to save for retirement or anything else for that matter. I have struggled with saving ever since because I never got into the habit of saving.

We did get out of debt, but I have many regrets. My creditors do not care that I sacrificed time with my family and friends to pay them, and my family was not happy that I put my creditors' demands before my family's needs. Furthermore, my savings toward retirement are insufficient.

Even though my husband and I were well educated and had good jobs, we didn't have the answers we needed to get out of debt and to avoid making all the financial mistakes we did, mistakes I warn you not to make in this book. That's my motivation for writing this book: to help you get out of debt and avoid the mistakes I made and most of my clients have made.

I've had personal experience of being in debt, and I spent my early career working for creditors, which taught me how creditors think and what they do. Creditors have a lot of money, and they spend a lot of it hiring the best marketers they can to get people into debt and to keep them in debt, and they hire the best attorneys they can to collect that debt. Creditors have done a masterful job of convincing the public that bankruptcy is to be avoided at all costs. I bought into that message, and it resulted in a divorce, unhappy children, and an estranged sister. I avoided bankruptcy, but it came at a terrible cost.

I'm not saying you shouldn't pay your debts if you can, but depriving your family to pay your creditors may not be the best solution. It concerns me that many financial advisors make bankruptcy out to be the "end of the world." Some of these advisors actually filed bankruptcy themselves but incredibly tell their clients to avoid doing so at all costs. Many very successful people will tell you that filing bankruptcy was one of their best decisions. They finally realized the lie that creditors want us all to believe, that "bankruptcy is the end." These successful people finally came to the realization they actually had nothing to fear, and they finally took the risks they needed to take to become extremely successful. My point is that you should consider all options to get out of debt, even bankruptcy.

I learned how creditors operated, and I saw attorneys allegedly trying to help people get out of debt be more concerned about helping themselves. While representing creditors, I would get calls from debtors represented by selfish attorneys begging me to help them keep their homes and property. The ethical rules for lawyers prevented me from being able even to talk with them. They would tell me their lawyers would not take their calls or would tell them there was nothing that could be done. These calls haunted me; those debtors needed help.

Finally, about twenty years ago, I realized that even if I had to take a big income hit, I needed to switch sides and help debtors with the procedure that creditors hate but is the most successful and cost-effective way to get out of debt—bankruptcy. In addition, we are the only bankruptcy law firm in the area to offer a program to help clients rebuild their credit so that 2 years after bankruptcy, they can qualify for a regular interest mortgage home loan. Over the years, I gathered the expertise I'm about to share with you in this book, which I wrote to help as many people as possible get out of debt in the best way possible.

INTRODUCTION

There comes a time when you realize it's time to deal with your debt once and for all. It's very difficult to deal with your debt if you're in a transitional period of your life such as a separation, divorce, job loss, medical problems, moving, and so on. In fact, it is often during transitions or other extraordinary events that most people find themselves getting into debt. Times of transition are usually not the best times to tackle debt problems. During transitions and other crises, your goal should probably be to stabilize your situation, including your cash flow. When things are finally stabilized and you have figured out a way to achieve a positive cash flow, that's the time to get serious about getting out of debt and exploring your options to do so.

This book will not explain how to budget (however, in the final chapter, I provide a budget form you could use), nor does it cover ways to get a positive cash flow situation. This book assumes that you have stabilized your cash flow so you are not going deeper into debt. Until your income exceeds your expenses, no technique—including bankruptcy—will get you out of debt. What good is a bankruptcy if you just get into debt again but can't get a Chapter 7 bankruptcy discharge for another eight years?

Debt Statistics

More than 160 million Americans have credit cards, and the average credit card holder has at least three cards. The overall average balance nationwide for credit cards is $7,300 (including those with and without balances). However, those households with credit card balances have average balances of $15,000. About 15 percent of American adults have been late making credit card payments, and 8 percent have missed at least one credit card payment entirely. About 4 percent are delinquent sixty or more days. New Yorkers typically carry credit card balances of only $6,600, but they have high student loan balances; the average graduates have student loan balances of more than $26,000. The average amount of student loan debt in New York works out to $4,600 per person. Nationwide, student loan debt exceeds $1 trillion, which is more than all the credit card and car loan debt in the United States.

In addition, 10 percent of New York mortgages are delinquent by more than three months and are at risk of foreclosure. In fact, the delinquency rate is higher only in Nevada (13.6 percent) and Florida (18 percent). The average total debt (including credit card, mortgage, home equity, student, car loans, and other loans) for all U.S. households with credit card debt is $54,000.

Every year, about 1 million individuals and couples file bankruptcy. The highest number, over 2 million, occurred in 2005 due to a law Congress passed that took effect near the end of 2005. In 2014, there were approximately 936,000 bankruptcy filings. In the last ten years, over 10 million households filed bankruptcy. Since there are approximately 115 million households in the United States, this means that more than one out of every ten households filed bankruptcy in those ten years.

Studies show that 46 percent of all bankruptcies are related to medical problems that resulted in medical bills plus lost work. However, more recently, the causes of bankruptcy have shifted more to job loss and reduced income. In addition, those with only some college are more likely to file bankruptcy because they have the burden of student loans but don't have the higher salaries those with degrees receive. The typical person filing for bankruptcy is older, married, has a high school education, and makes less than $30,000. However, the type of person who files more bankruptcies than any other is the single parent.

Reactions to Being in Debt

The most common reaction to being in debt is denial. No one wants to accept the truth about a bad situation; many hope that it will just go away. When a crisis hits, they use the crisis

Statistical information came from:
http://www.abiworld.org/Content/NavigationMenu/NewsRoom/BankruptcyStatistics/Bankruptcy_Filings_1.htm; http://www.debt.org/bankruptcy/statistics/; http://www.statisticbrain.com/credit-card-debt-statistics/; http://www.nerdwallet.com/blog/credit-card-data/average-credit-card-debt-household/; http://www.credit.com/press/statistics/student-credit-and-debt-statistics.html.

management principle of robbing Peter to pay Paul, which makes the situation worse. When reality does hit, their next reaction is stress; they become worried all the time, they can't fall asleep, and they may eat to distract themselves or use alcohol to escape the stress. The stress begins to affect their work, home, and other relationships.

Another common reaction is fear. Those deep in debt become afraid to answer the phone or open mail or even the door. They shun others because they cannot afford to do things with them. The fear affects their close relationships, and very often, this fear destroys these relationships. They withdraw and become depressed. They feel that their situations are hopeless and that things won't change. They get angry, blame themselves or their spouses for their situations, and may even consider suicide. None of this, however, solves anything.

To find relief, they have to look at the causes of their financial difficulties and create plans to deal with their debt.

THE BEST WAYS TO GET OUT OF DEBT

For Those in Debt

There is no one best way to get out of debt; the best way for you to do so may be very different from the best way for another person to solve the problem. The best way may be as simple or as complicated as your debt situation is.

Many financial advisors will offer you only one solution for helping you out of debt and not mention any options. The goal of this book is to give you the different options available to get out of debt and to offer suggestions about which may be the best for you considering your particular situation. Many "methods" to get out of debt are really just delaying strategies or ways of swapping one type of debt or creditor for another (i.e., unsecured debt to secured debt or debt consolidation) and will not get you out of debt.

The first thing you need to do to get out of debt is to get completely honest about your financial situation; the truth shall make you free. Figure out how much debt you really have. Get a free copy of your credit report at www.annualcreditreport. com/cra/index.jsp. Add any debts owed to family members or medical providers, and include house, car, furniture, and student loans. Also, include any taxes you owe to the IRS or New York State. You and your spouse need to be very honest with each other—no more hiding debts and financial problems from each other. Put it all down on paper.

You then need to look at your income and create a budget. Do you have sufficient income to pay your creditors? At the rate you can pay them, how long will it take you?

Factors to Consider

The different factors to consider in deciding which method to use to get out of debt include the following:

1. The amount of your debt

2. The types of your debt (secured, unsecured, student loans, taxes, judgments, etc.)

3. The amount and source of your income and whether it is steady or variable

4. The amount and source of expenses and whether required for survival or resulting from various types of debt

5. The amount and types of your assets (real estate, vehicles, retirement funds, toys such as snowmobiles), liquid assets (such as savings or stocks), and claims (such as personal injury settlements)

6. Your financial history and future (What caused the debt, and can or have things changed for the better or worse?)

Having worked for creditors for many years, I have learned that creditors analyze a debtor's situation from the base line of bankruptcy. Creditors fear bankruptcy because it can be such an effective method for someone to get out of debt to them. If a debtor does not file bankruptcy, the creditor will likely become more aggressive in collecting the debt. The creditor will reason that if the debtor doesn't file bankruptcy, it's because the debtor can't because they have assets that cannot be protected by bankruptcy or they make too much money to file bankruptcy. Of course, the creditor wants to be first in line to grab those assets or garnish that income. Therefore, just as the creditors look at bankruptcy as the baseline, I too start with bankruptcy.

I will start with the absolute best ways, which can work from 95 to 99 percent of the time, and then discuss other methods to consider if the best will not work. These next-best alternatives work about 25 to 50 percent of the time. The final options that I will discuss should be avoided except in extremely rare situations because these solutions work less than 10 percent of the time, and they come with significant problems. I will then discuss specific debt situations, including taxes, mortgage foreclosures/modifications, student loans, and military situations.

I will present the different ways to get out of debt primarily through the use of case studies using hypothetical people in different financial scenarios. None of these case studies is of any actual individual or couple I have represented or advised, of course, but I have used elements of my clients' situations to create some of these hypothetical situations. I also try to explain that if some of the facts presented were different, the outcome or solution could also change. This is why it is important to consult with a competent attorney on the facts of your particular case and be completely honest about your situation. Attorneys can always achieve better outcomes when they know the facts before rather than after you file bankruptcy.

I end the book with a section designed for professionals on how to use the factors to help individuals and couples figure out the best solution in differing situations.

Bankruptcy - Chapter 7

Every creditor knows that the best way for anyone to get out of debt is via a Chapter 7 bankruptcy, which works about 95 to 99 percent of the time. It costs only a small fraction of the debt, it's fast, and it's legal. That's why creditors do all they can to make bankruptcy sound as though it's the end of the world, but it isn't. It takes only two years after a bankruptcy before you can get a regular-interest home loan, and you can always get a car loan if you have a job and we offer a credit improvement program to help clients make this happen. Studies show that people who file bankruptcy will get more credit card offers than average Americans; creditors get names and addresses off bankruptcy rolls to send credit offers to because they know those on that list cannot file for bankruptcy for eight years. The creditors' dirty little secret is that they make most of their money from people who need to file bankruptcy or who have just filed bankruptcy. People who need to file bankruptcy or who have just filed bankruptcy pay interest, late fees, over-the-limit fees, and any other fees creditors can come up with. The creditors don't make as much money off all those who pay their credit card debts in full every month. The 2005 bankruptcy bill was crafted in large part to delay bankruptcy filings so creditors could collect several more months of interest and other charges.

Most people think that those who file bankruptcy are irresponsible with money, but this is a huge myth. The reality is that most people who need to file bankruptcy have suffered one or more major and unexpected financial setbacks in their lives such as divorces, separations, job losses, and serious health problems that all of a sudden push their income levels down drastically and unexpectedly. A recent study showed that about half of all bankruptcies are the result of medical issues; these debtors often struggle for years before finally accepting the fact that they need to file bankruptcy.

As far as I know, none of my clients ever planned in advance to file bankruptcy, and I never want to represent someone who plans in advance to do so. My clients always struggle with the decision to file, and they try a variety of alternatives (most of them a waste of time and money) before they actually file bankruptcy. The number-one type of person filing bankruptcy is the single parent, and I think this is because single parents quickly realize that the needs of their families are far more important than the demands of the creditors. Although creditors have done a great job of convincing the world that bankruptcy is a terrible thing, I am grateful our forefathers provided for bankruptcy in the U.S. Constitution. I suspect they realized that freedom included the ability to have economic freedom.

Case History: David and Brenda Nelson

David, who works as a roofer, makes good money during the roofing season, which starts usually in April and continues through October.

Lately, however, the roofing season has been much shorter, and not as many people are redoing their roofs. During the winter months, David relies on unemployment, which is really tough, because their heating bills are high at that time. Brenda works as an administrative assistant. They have two children, both in school. Before the children started school, however, Brenda worked during the winter months or babysat other children.

Brenda and David wanted a parent to be home with the children before the children started school. They didn't always have health insurance, but Brenda's job fortunately provides it. They owe quite a bit in old medical bills and a lot in credit card bills. They ran up their credit cards when David was not working. They usually use their tax refunds to get current on their utilities, buy clothes for the children, and get their cars repaired. Being behind on their credit card and medical bills has, however, ruined their credit. They really want to be able to buy a home and will need to buy another vehicle soon.

Summary of Financial Case:

Married

Husband's income: $17,500/year for roofing, $11,856/year for unemployment

Wife's income: $29,126/year

Total income: $58,482/year

Tax refunds: $3,200/year

Two dependents

Rent

2010 Chevy Malibu: balance $4,545, value $5,200, $300/month payment

2003 Chevy Truck: paid for, value $3,000

Five credit cards: $38,000, latest charges were for Christmas gifts and gas purchases in winter

Six medical bills: $6,300

One personal loan: $1,200

Total unsecured debt: $45,500

No student loans, no tax debt, no child support, no judgments, no cosigners, no gambling losses, no businesses within last six years, and no prior bankruptcy cases

Bankruptcy is the fastest and least expensive way for a couple or individual to get out of debt. Bankruptcy is a perfect solution for the Nelson family because their income has stabilized and they have health insurance. They can use their tax refunds to pay bankruptcy costs. They qualify for a Chapter 7 bankruptcy based on their income and the type of debt they have. They can get another car loan once their bankruptcy is over, and in about two years, they can qualify for a normal interest rate mortgage loan.

Documents they will need to file bankruptcy:

- Social Security cards

- Driver's licenses

- Last two years' tax returns

- Seven months of pay stubs and unemployment payments for both

- Titles to vehicle they own

- Car payoff statement for the vehicle they owe on

- All credit card, medical, and personal loan bills and collection letters

The timing of their case is important. The new bankruptcy law says that the last six months of the debtors' income is doubled to determine if they qualify under the "means test" or income test to file a Chapter 7 bankruptcy. If David's roofing income had been extremely good during the summer and they filed just after summer, under the six-month rule, the couple's income might be too high, and they could be found to have made too much money to file a Chapter 7. They probably should try to file bankruptcy in the spring, when David's income for the prior six months would be at the lowest level.

It is critical to be very honest with your bankruptcy attorney before you file bankruptcy. It's sometimes impossible to get out of bankruptcy after you file, and you could end up losing assets we could have protected if we'd known about them in advance. Furthermore, it's a bankruptcy crime not to disclose everything required by bankruptcy law. If in doubt about something, discuss it with your bankruptcy attorney as soon as possible and before you file.

Let's look at the factors listed above to understand why a Chapter 7 bankruptcy solution is a good solution for the Nelsons:

First, the amount of their debt is relatively high considering their income. It would require payments of over $1,000/ month for five years to pay off the unsecured debt, assuming an average interest rate of 15 percent. Assuming a ten-year payout, it would require payments of over $730/ month. We normally do not recommend bankruptcy if unsecured debt is less than $10,000.

Second, the type of debt the Nelsons have is primarily unsecured, which can be easily discharged in bankruptcy.

Third, the income for the Nelson family has increased and stabilized to the point that it's enough to take care of their ongoing expenses.

Fourth, their anticipated expenses will also likely be paid with their income after bankruptcy.

Fifth, their assets, chiefly their equity in their vehicles, would be protected in bankruptcy.

Sixth, their current and future financial situation looks great. They now have reliable medical insurance, the lack of which had caused part of their debt. Mrs. Nelson is now working full time, so their household income has increased and will be steadier. Filing bankruptcy will provide the Nelsons the fastest way to get the home they want since after bankruptcy, any extra income can be saved for a down payment on a home rather than used to pay off old bills. Plus with our credit improvement program, they know exactly what they need to successfully regain their credit.

Every case is different, and if we add different facts to this case, it may be difficult to impossible for the Nelsons to file bankruptcy. For example, if the Nelsons had paid off a debt of thousands of dollars to a family member from a tax refund, filing for bankruptcy would probably need to be delayed a year; otherwise, a bankruptcy trustee would pursue that family member to recover the amount repaid so it could be redistributed to the other creditors.

If the credit card debt were student loans, then a Chapter 7 bankruptcy would not be a good choice because student loans are non-dischargeable in bankruptcy. If the Nelsons inherited a home but transferred it to a relative so creditors couldn't take it, that transfer would be considered fraudulent and the bankruptcy trustee, someone appointed by the court to oversee bankruptcy cases, could undo the transfer and sell the home to pay creditors. It is important to talk with a competent and experienced bankruptcy attorney to make sure bankruptcy is the right option for you.

If an individual or couple can qualify for a Chapter 7 bankruptcy, the likelihood of successfully discharging liabilities is about 99 percent when they are represented by competent bankruptcy counsel.

Our firm has been helping individuals and couples in the central New York region file bankruptcy for over twenty years. Our office has helped over 10,000 individuals file bankruptcy.

In order for the Nelsons to qualify for a home loan in approximately two years, there are certain steps they should take during the bankruptcy and for two years after. Our office offers a post-bankruptcy credit improvement program that's like physical therapy after a major medical operation. The goal of the program is to help clients to firm up their financial situations so they can qualify for home loans two years after bankruptcy. This program, however, does not work for every debtor and it does require work and follow through on the debtor's part.

Add Upon Repayment Plan

The add upon repayment (also known as the snowball) strategy probably works less than 50 percent of the time in helping people get out of debt because it takes a lot of discipline. However, it is the most cost-effective and fastest method to get out of debt if you have to pay your creditors in full.

Case History: Steven and Jennifer Page

Steven is an artist, and Jennifer is physician working in an emergency room. They have no children. Jennifer makes about $175,000/year, and Steven, after expenses, has a slight negative income. Jennifer received a $5,000 bonus for taking her hospital job, and they keep that in savings for emergencies. However, getting through medical school caused Jennifer to incur a significant amount in student loans— about $150,000. They also bought a home, and they're paying on two cars. In addition, they have a furniture loan and some credit card debt they incurred when they moved for her new job.

Summary of Financial Case:

Married

Wife's income: $175,000/year

Husband's income: –$5,000/year (negative)

Total income: $170,000/year

Tax Refunds: $200/year

No Dependents

Home: balance $200,000, value $200,000, $2,100/month payment

2014 Honda Accord: balance $24,545, value $23,200, $450/month payment

2012 Nissan Cube: balance $15,000, value $13,000, $350/month payment

Furniture loan: balance $5,990, $250/month payment

Five credit cards: balance $36,000; $460/month minimum payments

Student loans: balance $150,000, $1,500/month payment

Total unsecured debt: $186,000

No tax debt, no child support, no judgments, no cosigners, no gambling losses, and no prior bankruptcy cases.

Because of their high income, this couple is better off paying off their debts. The best way to pay off debts is using what I call the add upon repayment method. To make this work, it is critical that they do not go into more debt, so there must be some savings to cover "emergencies" before they use this method. As well, their income must be stable enough to make regular payments. Finally, income must continue to exceed expenses for this method to work.

There are two basic ways to do the add upon repayment method. The first is to pay the smallest balances off first and pay off the larger balances next, while the other is to focus on paying off the debts with the highest interest rates. You will pay off the debt faster by focusing on the balances with the highest interest rates, but you'll receive more motivation by paying off the smaller balances first and watching the number of your creditors diminish. You start with payments as low as the minimum payments, and when you pay off one balance, you add the payment you were making on it to the payment you're making to another debt. Here I used the calculator at www.free-online-calculator-use.com/rapid-debt-reduction-calculator.html. The first set of totals show the amount the Pages would pay in interest ($73,472.53) if they paid only the minimum payments, and it would take 224 months—eighteen and a half years. The second total shows the amount of interest they would pay under the add upon repayment method ($44,063.81), and it would take 92 months—seven and a half years.

Creditor	Loan Balance	Interest Rate	Monthly Pmts	Interest Cost	# of Pmts Left
1. Honda Fnc	24,545	3.99	450	2,583	61
2. Nissan Fnc	15,000	4	350	1,213	47
3. Furniture	5,990	9	250	638	27
4. Visa 1	6,000	13	75	8,025	187
5. Visa 2	7,500	15	100	14,819	224
6. MC 1	10,000	12	125	10,219	162
7. MC 2	8,000	11	85	10,499	218
8. MC 3	4,500	18	75	7,099	155
9. Student Loan	150,000	2.5	1500	18,378	113
Totals	$231,535	start at $3,010		$73,473	224 months
Snowball	$231,535	continue $3,010		$44,064	92 months
Savings	$29,409	132 saved months			

If the Pages could add another $1,000 a month to their payments, the debts would be paid in sixty-five months, less than five and a half years, and that's 159 months or thirteen and a quarter years in saved time. In addition, it would save them $45,885.98 in interest.

The payment schedule would be as follows if they started and stayed with the minimum payment amount of $3,010:

Pmt	Date	Debt 1	Debt 2	Debt 3	Debt 4	Debt 5	Debt 6	Debt 7	Debt 8	Debt 9
1	Oct 2012	450	350	250	75	100	125	85	75	1,500
2	Nov 2012	450	350	250	75	100	125	85	75	1,500
3	Dec 2012	450	350	250	75	100	125	85	75	1,500
4	Jan 2013	450	350	250	75	100	125	85	75	1,500
5	Feb 2013	450	350	250	75	100	125	85	75	1,500
6	Mar 2013	450	350	250	75	100	125	85	75	1,500
7	Apr 2013	450	350	250	75	100	125	85	75	1,500
8	May 2013	450	350	250	75	100	125	85	75	1,500
9	Jun 2013	450	350	250	75	100	125	85	75	1,500
10	Jul 2013	450	350	250	75	100	125	85	75	1,500
11	Aug 2013	450	350	250	75	100	125	85	75	1,500
12	Sep 2013	450	350	250	75	100	125	85	75	1,500
13	Oct 2013	450	350	250	75	100	125	85	75	1,500
14	Nov 2013	450	350	250	75	100	125	85	75	1,500
15	Dec 2013	450	350	250	75	100	125	85	75	1,500
16	Jan 2014	450	350	250	75	100	125	85	75	1,500
17	Feb 2014	450	350	250	75	100	125	85	75	1,500
18	Mar 2014	450	350	250	75	100	125	85	75	1,500
19	Apr 2014	450	350	250	75	100	125	85	75	1,500
20	May 2014	450	350	250	75	100	125	85	75	1,500
21	Jun 2014	450	350	250	75	100	125	85	75	1,500

22	Jul 2014	450	350	250	75	100	125	85	75	1,500
23	Aug 2014	450	350	250	75	100	125	85	75	1,500
24	Sep 2014	450	350	250	75	100	125	85	75	1,500
25	Oct 2014	450	350	250	75	100	125	85	75	1,500
26	Nov 2014	450	350	250	75	100	125	85	75	1,500
27	Dec 2014	572	350	128	75	100	125	85	75	1,500
28	Jan 2015	700	350		75	100	125	85	75	1,500
29	Feb 2015	700	350		75	100	125	85	75	1,500
30	Mar 2015	700	350		75	100	125	85	75	1,500
31	Apr 2015	700	350		75	100	125	85	75	1,500
32	May 2015	700	350		75	100	125	85	75	1,500
33	Jun 2015	700	350		75	100	125	85	75	1,500
34	Jul 2015	700	350		75	100	125	85	75	1,500
35	Aug 2015	700	350		75	100	125	85	75	1,500
36	Sep 2015	700	350		75	100	125	85	75	1,500
37	Oct 2015	700	350		75	100	125	85	75	1,500
38	Nov 2015	700	350		75	100	125	85	75	1,500
39	Dec 2015	700	350		75	100	125	85	75	1,500
40	Jan 2016	700	350		75	100	125	85	75	1,500
41	Feb 2016	700	350		75	100	125	85	75	1,500
42	Mar 2016	700	350		75	100	125	85	75	1,500
43	Apr 2016	700	350		75	100	125	85	75	1,500
44	May 2016	700	350		75	100	125	85	75	1,500
45	Jun 2016	700	350		75	100	125	85	75	1,500
46	Jul 2016	700	350		75	100	125	85	75	1,500
47	Aug 2016	937	113		75	100	125	85	75	1,500
48	Sep 2016	310			815	100	125	85	75	1,500
49	Oct 2016				1,125	100	125	85	75	1,500
50	Nov 2016				1,125	100	125	85	75	1,500

51	Dec 2016	1,125	100	125	85	75	1,500
52	Jan 2017	1,125	100	125	85	75	1,500
53	Feb 2017	268	957	125	85	75	1,500
54	Mar 2017		1,225	125	85	75	1,500
55	Apr 2017		1,225	125	85	75	1,500
56	May 2017		1,225	125	85	75	1,500
57	Jun 2017		1,225	125	85	75	1,500
58	Jul 2017		1,225	125	85	75	1,500
59	Aug 2017		297	1,053	85	75	1,500
60	Sep 2017			1,350	85	75	1,500
61	Oct 2017			1,350	85	75	1,500
62	Nov 2017			1,350	85	75	1,500
63	Dec 2017			1,350	85	75	1,500
64	Jan 2018			1,350	85	75	1,500
65	Feb 2018			555	880	75	1,500
66	Mar 2018				1,435	75	1,500
67	Apr 2018				1,435	75	1,500
68	May 2018				1,435	75	1,500
69	Jun 2018				1,435	75	1,500
70	Jul 2018				591	920	1,500
71	Aug 2018					1,510	1,500
72	Sep 2018					1,288	1,722
73	Oct 2018						3,010
74	Nov 2018						3,010
75	Dec 2018						3,010
76	Jan 2019						3,010
77	Feb 2019						3,010

78	Mar 2019	3,010
79	Apr 2019	3,010
80	May 2019	3,010
81	Jun 2019	3,010
82	Jul 2019	3,010
83	Aug 2019	3,010
84	Sep 2019	3,010
85	Oct 2019	3,010
86	Nov 2019	3,010
87	Dec 2019	3,010
88	Jan 2020	3,010
89	Feb 2020	3,010
90	Mar 2020	3,010
91	Apr 2020	3,010
92	May 2020	1,689

Documents needed for the add upon repayment option:

- Pay stubs reflecting typical and anticipated income

- Anticipated business budget for Mr. Page

- Payoff statements for all debts

- All bills and initial loan contracts reflecting the interest rates for each debt and the minimum monthly payments

- Credit report

- List of anticipated new expenses during the payment plan period

- Savings to cover future emergencies

- Budget showing a positive cash flow sufficient to cover plan payments

Let's look at these factors to understand why repayment of debt, not bankruptcy, is the best solution for the Pages. First, although the amount of their debt is high, they have a high income, which would make them ineligible for a Chapter 7; they would need to file a Chapter 13. The estimated payments in a Chapter 13 would be higher than those in an add upon repayment plan. They also are not confined by the requirements of Chapter 13, which include a prohibition on any more debt.

Second, a large portion of the Page's debt is student loans, which cannot be discharged in bankruptcy, so it doesn't make economic sense for them to file bankruptcy.

Third, their income has increased and stabilized; it's enough to take care of ongoing expenses and pay off their debt. They also have savings to cover emergencies, so they likely won't need to go into more debt.

Fourth, the Pages can afford their on-going expenses.

Fifth, the Pages do not have a lot of equity in their assets.

Sixth, their current and future financial situation looks great. They have made it through medical school and an expensive move that caused a large part of their debt. Dr. Page is working full time, so the household's income has increased and will likely increase.

If their debt were related to the husband's failed business, say, rather than student loans, they might want to consider a Chapter 7 bankruptcy. The bankruptcy code allows debtors with failed-business debt to file a Chapter 7 bankruptcy even if their income might support a Chapter 13.

The success rate for the add upon repayment strategy is probably less than 50 percent since it can take many years to complete the plan, and so many things can happen to derail the program. The success rate would increase if a financial coach were around to help a couple or individual stay committed.

Our office can meet with clients to set up this program and provide ongoing coaching to help increase the likelihood of success through using this program.

SECOND-BEST CHOICES

Bankruptcy - Chapter 13

Chapter 13 is often called a wage earner's plan because in the Chapter 13 plan, the debtor pays all or a portion of the debt from his/her wages. Chapter 13 bankruptcies work only about 50 percent of the time. You are in a Chapter 13 bankruptcy for at least three but usually five years. You are prohibited from buying or selling assets or getting credit during that time without bankruptcy court approval. Chapter 13 requires creditors to accept the plan as long as it meets the bankruptcy code's requirements. We believe that a Chapter 7 is usually the best alternative, but sometimes a Chapter 13 is required, or it provides better cash flow, or it is better in cases in which the debtors' financial future is extremely unpredictable. Furthermore, since the plan payments come directly from the debtors' wages, it has a higher success rate than if the plan payments were "voluntary."

Case History: James and Stacey O'Brien

James is a police officer with a good income; in the past, he had a lot of overtime, but that's currently unavailable. Stacey is a stay-at-home mom. The O'Briens decided to get a second mortgage

to consolidate their debt so Stacey could stay at home with their child. Like most people trying to consolidate debt, they find that they just continue to turn to the credit cards for all the unexpected expenses and find themselves in the hole again.

The O'Briens could afford the second mortgage payment while James was getting overtime, but now they cannot afford the second mortgage, and to make matters worse, the decline in home values has caused the O'Briens to now owe more on their house than it's worth, so they can't sell it. Since the second mortgage holder was bugging them about the payment, they paid the second mortgage payments by missing two payments on the first mortgage. Now, the first mortgage holder is threatening foreclosure if they miss another payment—so robbing Peter to pay Paul caught up with them. If they miss another first mortgage payment, the mortgage company will not accept additional payments except the full amount necessary to make the mortgage completely current.

They also needed a newer car a few years ago, but they still owed a significant amount on their existing car loan. The car dealer arranged for the unpaid balance on the old car to be added to the balance due on the new car, so as is the case with their house, they now owe more on the car than it's worth.

When times were better, they bought a four-wheeler to plow their driveway, and they want to keep it if possible.

Finally, they got behind on their credit card bills, and one of the creditors filed a judgment against Stacey, which means there's a judgment lien on their home as well.

Summary of Financial Case:

Married

Husband's income: $65,000/year

Wife's income: $0

Total income: $65,000/year

Tax refunds: $1,400/year

One dependent

Home: value $92,000, first mortgage balance $95,000, $900/month payment, two payments behind; second mortgage balance $25,000, $350/month payment, several payments behind

Dodge Caravan: balance $17,000, value $12,200, $450/month payment

2003 Honda Civic: paid for, value $3,000

2014 four-wheeler: paid for, value $4,000

Ten credit and store cards: $45,500 (latest charges were for car repairs)

Two medical bills: $1,100

Total unsecured debt: $46,600

No student loans, no tax debt, no child support, no judgments, no cosigners, no gambling losses, no businesses within last six years, and no prior bankruptcy cases.

A Chapter 13 repayment plan is the best option for the O'Briens. A Chapter 13 will allow the O'Briens to retain their home and vehicles plus lower their monthly expenses. It will also put the O'Briens in a better equity position on their assets.

Documents needed to file for bankruptcy.

- Social Security cards

- Driver's licenses

- Last two years of tax returns

- Seven months of pay stubs, if any, for husband and wife

- Recorded deed and recorded mortgages on their home

- Mortgage payoff statements

- Titles for Honda Civic and Dodge Caravan

- Purchase documents for the four-wheeler

- Dodge Caravan payoff statement

- Mortgage statement which includes the amount of arrears

- Lawsuit paperwork from judgment creditor

- All credit card bills, medical bills, and collection letters

Let's look at these factors to understand why a Chapter 13 bankruptcy is a good solution for the O'Briens.

First, bankruptcy is a good solution because the amount of their debt is relatively high, especially considering the negative equity situation in their house and the car. It would require payments of over $1,800/month for five years to pay off the unsecured debt, assuming an average interest rate of 15 percent, if they didn't file bankruptcy. A ten-year pay out would require payments of over $1,200/month.

Second, a Chapter 13 plan can help the O'Briens restructure their debt in some powerful ways. In a Chapter 13 plan, the second mortgage can be eliminated as a mortgage and treated as an unsecured claim in the bankruptcy plan. Also, in a Chapter 13 bankruptcy, the O'Briens can put the two months of mortgage arrears of the first mortgage into the Chapter 13 plan and go on making their regular monthly mortgage payments. Because of the age of the car loan, it can be "crammed down" so the O'Briens pay only the value ($12,200) of the car back in the bankruptcy plan rather than the amount owed, $17,000. As well, the judgment lien can be eliminated in the bankruptcy and the judgment claim treated as an unsecured creditor. In addition, they can consolidate their significant amount of unsecured debt and pay back a relatively small portion in a Chapter 13 plan.

Third, the O'Brien family income has decreased because of the lack of overtime but is otherwise steady. However, the $65,000/year income is still near the median amount of income earned by a family of three in New York. The U.S. bankruptcy trustee will likely object if the O'Briens try to file a Chapter 7 rather than Chapter 13 since there is some excess income to make some payment toward the unsecured debt. In other words, there is sufficient income to fund a Chapter 13 plan.

Fourth, the O'Briens' expenses are not unusual, and they can afford the Chapter 13 plan payment. In fact, in the Chapter 13 plan, their expenses will decrease because they don't have to pay the second mortgage, they can reduce their car payment because of the cram down, and the payoff will increase to a five-year repayment period. The bankruptcy also prevents the judgment creditor from garnishing the debtors' wages.

Fifth, the O'Briens' assets would be protected in a bankruptcy. The bankruptcy exemptions would protect the equity in the O'Briens' vehicles. Having a four-wheeler in a Chapter 7 case can sometimes be a problem in that the court may consider it a luxury item and may try to sell it to pay other creditors. In a Chapter 13, debtors may keep "luxury items" or things they cannot protect in a Chapter 7 case.

Sixth, the O'Briens' current and future financial situation looks steady. A Chapter 13 bankruptcy would help lower their monthly expenses and increase the equity in their assets. A Chapter 13 bankruptcy would eliminate the second mortgage (with its $350/month payment) and judgment lien on their home. It would pay off the Caravan in five years at a lower payment (about $260/month rather than $450/month). The O'Briens would also pay just a portion of the unsecured debt, maybe 10 percent or less.

Chapter 13 cases are very difficult because the plans are at least three years long and usually last for five years. Again, a well-established and experienced bankruptcy lawyer is needed since those filing Chapter 13s want to make sure the bankruptcy lawyer will be there if the economics of the household change over the next five years (and don't most household's income and expenses change over a five-year period?) The plan may need to be modified if Stacey goes back to work, if she has another child, or for a host of other possibilities.

Again, if we change the facts so that the O'Briens did not have negative equity in their home and car, we might suggest trying a Chapter 7.

Because there can be so many changes over a five-year period, only about 50 percent of Chapter 13 cases result in successful discharge of liabilities, so having experienced bankruptcy counsel is critical in proceeding with a Chapter 13 bankruptcy case. Keep in mind that not all attorneys know all the options for Chapter 13 or how to implement them.

Negotiating with Creditors

This strategy rarely works over the long run and is an extremely frustrating strategy, but it can provide some temporary help. Creditors analyze your situation based on how likely it is you will file a bankruptcy; if you are making your payments, they believe you won't file, and so they have no reason to change the arrangements. Another problem is finding someone on behalf of the creditor who has authority to accept your proposal. Some have authority to accept a change in payment for one or two months but not permanent changes. Many creditors will simply not respond to your requests for changes; most will want you to pay more than you offer, so make sure you have room to negotiate if you are going to try this strategy.

In using this strategy, work like a broken record—politely ask for what you want again and again. If the person you are talking with cannot or will not help you, politely hang up and try another person; this strategy sometimes helps. Another strategy is to ask for the supervisor and then the supervisor's supervisor, going up the chain of command.

Never, never promise something unless you know you can fulfill that promise. If they demand something you cannot do, tell them you can't do it. Don't assume you're going to win the lottery and will be able to pay them what they demand, and do not steal from Peter to pay Paul. Make sure you can cover your regular obligations before you offer to pay them something. You want to make sure you stay consistent and reliable as possible. If you can't fulfill the terms of your new proposal, they will stop working with you and start aggressive collection efforts.

Try to work with the original creditors if possible. Be proactive with a plan rather than wait for them to contact you. However, be careful what you tell them. Never lie, but don't reveal to them all your resources. If creditors become rude on the phone, tell them politely you can no longer discuss the matter in a way that is helpful to both sides, tell them you are going to hang up, and hang up. If a creditor tries to intimate that you are a "bad" person because you cannot pay them, don't fall for the bait. You can tell them you are contacting them to try to work out a win-win agreement but you can do only what you can. If necessary, politely tell them you cannot discuss the matter with them; hang up, call again, and speak to another person or a supervisor.

Unsecured creditors (involving credit cards, medical bills, and other loans) will be less likely to agree to negotiate if you use an attorney or other professional. The creditors will think that if you can afford to pay an attorney, you can afford to pay your bills. When I have tried negotiation on behalf of clients, most of the creditors ignore my offers or want more than the clients can afford. Furthermore, attorneys' fees for this type of negotiation far exceed the cost to file bankruptcy and only add to the debt burden. However, if you are attempting to negotiate on a large secured debt such as a mortgage or a large tax debt, then you will be more successful by using an attorney.

Don't expect a reduction in the amount you owe a creditor. You can and should ask for that, but don't expect it. You might be able to expect a temporary reduction in payment or a temporary reduction in the interest rate. If you want a reduction in the amount you owe a creditor, you must be prepared to pay that creditor the entire reduced amount immediately.

Remember when you negotiate to make sure that they protect your credit score if that's important to you. If you get any agreement, make sure it's in writing and signed by the other side. You can prepare a written agreement to send them for their signature. At a minimum, you should send a letter outlining what you understand the agreement to be and send it certified mail, return receipt requested, or if you are sending the agreement by email, send it in a manner that you know they opened the email, or send it by fax and retain the record that the fax was received.

Case History: Paul and Deborah Babcock

Paul works as a computer programmer, making $45,000/year, and Deborah is a secretary, making $30,000/year. They have two children and owe $85,000 on a house with a value of $125,000. He drives a 2003 Honda Civic, which is paid off, and his wife drives a 2014 Kia Sorento minivan on which they owe $5,000. They owe about $4,000 for furniture they bought the previous year.

Paul had a serious accident at home; he fell off a ladder and broke his wrist. He's unable to work, and the doctor has indicated it may take three months before he can use his wrist at work. Paul didn't have disability insurance, except what New York State provides, and they don't have much in savings. They can make mortgage payments and pay for ongoing expenses on Deborah's salary, but they don't have the funds to pay the full car payment and the furniture loan.

Summary of Financial Case:

Married

Husband's income: $45,000/year or $3,750/month but only $500/month while on New York State disability

Wife's income: $30,000/year

Two dependents

Home: balance $85,000, value $125,000, $920/month payment

2014 Kia Sorento: balance $5,000, value $10,000, $500/month payment

2003 Honda Civic: paid for, value $4,000

Furniture loan: balance $4,000, $275/month payment

No student loans, no tax debt, no child support, no judgments, no cosigners, no gambling losses, no businesses within the last six years, and no prior bankruptcy cases.

Documents they should have to negotiate with creditors:

- Wife's pay stubs

- Proof of husband's disability income

- Doctor's report and estimate of the time before husband can return to work

Since this financial crisis will last only about three months, the Babcocks should try to negotiate with their car and furniture lenders for some temporary relief. They should explain their circumstances to the car lender and ask to be able to pay the interest only for four months; payments should not be more than about $50 based on the fact they have been paying $500/month for over five years already. The car lender may agree to only two months with a review after that.

 The Babcocks should request a complete waiver of a need to make any payments or make payments of just $25/month for four months on the furniture loan. Again, they need to provide the lenders some proof of the situation. In addition, the Babcocks need to understand that this will not get them out of making all the payments; it only extends the time it will take them to pay off their debts. If the creditors will not initially agree, they should try discussing the matter with the supervisor and remind them that they have a history of making timely payments. They should also continue calling until they get the relief they need. Creditors have no obligation to agree to the arrangement, but it is certainly worth trying. In addition, creditors will appreciate the fact that the

Babcocks are staying in contact with them and offering possible solutions.

Factors why the Babcocks should try negotiation:

First, the amount of their debt is relatively low, especially the debt that would be dischargeable in a bankruptcy.

Second, most of the Babcocks' debt is secured by the house and car, and there is equity to support the debt.

Third, the Babcocks' income is temporarily low but should recover after a few months, allowing them to develop a plan to deal with the situation until Paul returns to work and they can go back to making regular payments.

Fourth, their temporary loss of income will end in a few months.

Fifth, although the Babcocks' assets would be protected in a bankruptcy, this is not the determining factor in this case.

We are willing to coach clients who want to negotiate with creditors. If the debt is a large debt such as a mortgage or taxes, we could represent the debtor. If the debtor is trying to negotiate with many smaller creditors such as credit cards or medical bills, it is better for the debtor to negotiate directly and check with a coach to review any offers.

Consumer Credit Counseling

Credit counseling works about 25 to 50 percent of the time. Consumer credit services are "free" because funding comes from credit card companies, so credit counseling companies' loyalty is to the credit card companies, not the individual seeking such counseling. One IRS person investigating these types of companies has called them "disguised collection agencies." Because you think these credit counseling companies are your "friends," you will disclose resources (i.e., retirement funds, the possibility of getting a second mortgage, borrowing from relatives, etc.) you would never disclose to a collection agency. The credit counseling company then suggests that you use these resources in the credit card company's best interests, not yours. Credit counseling services work basically for credit card companies; they don't reduce how much you owe but simply forward your money to the credit card companies after they take some fees for themselves.

Credit counseling companies cannot help you with secured debt such as your mortgage, car payments, tax debt, child support debt, or judgments. These services report to the credit card companies and to the credit reporting companies that you are working with them, and so creditors will not grant credit during that time. Most of our clients who have worked with credit counseling services report that after months of struggling to pay these services, they have seen no decrease in the amount they owe. If possible, use the add upon repayment method before deciding to use consumer credit counseling.

Case History: Richard and Tammy Campbell

Richard, a technician, makes about $45,000/year, and Tammy, a schoolteacher, makes $56,000/year. They have two children. Tammy is fairly good with money, but Richard likes to spend. They have many arguments over money and blame each other when their bills don't get paid on time. They are constantly paying late fees and bank overdraft fees. They have a modest

home and two cars with a moderate balance on each. They have fifteen credit and store cards, and because of the late and missed payments, the interest charges are now 20 to 30 percent on each card, and they owe $33,000 on these cards. They have no money in savings, and Tammy's income varies because she doesn't get paid during the summer months.

Summary of Financial Case:

Married

Husband's income: $45,000/year

Wife's income: $56,000/year

Total income: $101,000/year

Tax refunds: $2,400/year

Two dependents

Home: balance $64,000, value $75,000, current on house, $750/month payment

2009 Ford Focus: balance $3,600, value $7,500, $300/month payment

2010 Kia Sedona: balance $5,500, value $8,300, $295/month payment

Fifteen credit and store cards: $33,000

No student loans, no tax debt, no child support obligations, no judgments, no cosigners, no gambling losses, no businesses within the last six years, and no prior bankruptcies.

Documents needed to work with consumer credit counseling:

- Pay stubs with typical anticipated income

- Payoff amounts for cars and house

- All bills

- Credit report

Let's analyze why consumer credit counseling may be the best solution for the Campbells. First, the amount of their debt is high, and they need to come up with a plan and take action. If the amount of debt were the only issue, bankruptcy would be a good solution.

Second, their debt is the type that could be discharged in bankruptcy, but again this is not the determining issue in this case.

Third, bankruptcy is not a great solution because the Campbells make too much money to file a Chapter 7 bankruptcy. They could file a Chapter 13 bankruptcy, but they would need to pay their creditors in full and would have to pay them at a rate they would likely find very difficult, especially given Richard's spending habits. The snowball strategy would not work well because the Campbells don't have any savings to use in emergencies and they don't have steady enough income.

Fourth, their expenses are such that they can afford to make payments to support a consumer credit counseling plan.

Fifth, the type of assets they have would be protected in a bankruptcy. Because the Campbells don't have any savings, the snowball method will not work.

Sixth, consumer credit counseling (CCC) might be a good solution because it can provide a plan and offer the couple third-party, impartial opinions and advice. Because Richard likes to spend money, he and Tammy cannot agree on a plan. Instead of Tammy just complaining and blaming the situation on Richard, CCC can be a neutral third party to let the couple learn what they are doing wrong financially. The Campbells could put together a budget and agree on a payment plan with CCC's help; CCC would take over getting the Campbells' payments to their creditors and might be able to reduce their interest rates. Using CCC services will be reported to the Campbell's credit reports and will restrict the Campbell's ability to get credit in the future, which might benefit this couple, although it may make it more difficult and expensive for them to get a car loan later.

In conclusion, if the couple makes too much money to file a Chapter 7, cannot agree on a plan, do not have the necessary savings for the snowball strategy, have default interest rates to pay, and need to reduce the ability to get additional credit, consumer credit counseling might be the best solution.

The success rate for most credit counseling companies is less than 50 percent. Because the plan is voluntary and because it lasts several years, too many problems can derail the plan.

Reverse-Mortgage Strategy

Many individuals and couples near retirement find that the net value of their assets has increased, but they are facing income decreases. This situation may make it impractical to file a bankruptcy. Those in retirement still need their assets, but they don't have the income to pay off unsecured debt. One solution may be a reverse mortgage.

A reverse mortgage is a loan against your home that you do not have to pay back as long as you live there. The loan proceeds can be paid to you all at once, as a regular monthly advance, or at times and in amounts of your choosing. The lender gets the money back plus interest when you die, sell your home, or permanently move out of it.

Reverse-mortgage borrowers continue to own their homes, so they still bear responsibility for property taxes, insurance, repairs, and so on. If they fail to carry out these responsibilities, their loans could become due and payable in full.

All borrowers must be at least sixty-two years old for most reverse mortgages. Owners generally must occupy the home as a principal residence (living there the majority of the year). Reverse-mortgage lenders are less concerned about the creditworthiness of the borrower; they are more concerned about how much equity the borrower has in his or her home.

Because reverse-mortgage borrowers make no monthly payments, the amount they owe grows over time, so the amount they have left after selling the home and paying off the loan (their "equity") generally grows smaller.

Case History: Elizabeth McBride

Retired home owner Elizabeth, sixty-eight, owns a home worth $175,000 on which she owes $25,000, but the payments are relatively high given the balance due since she has only a few years before the balance is paid in full. She receives about $1,500/month in Social Security and another $1,000 from her late husband's retirement. Her husband died about a year ago, and she experienced a loss of income as a result. She has tried to make do by using credit cards, but she realizes she cannot continue that. She currently owes about $15,000 on her cards. She has a reliable 2011 Honda Accord with less than 35,000 miles, but she owes $5,000 on it, and again the payments are relatively high since she has only eighteen months before this is paid in full.

Financial Summary:

Widow

Income: $30,000/year

Tax refund: nominal

No dependents

Home: worth $175,000, mortgage $25,000, $950/month payment

2011 Honda Accord: balance $5,000, value $13,000, $300/month payment

Credit card debt: $15,000

No student loans, no tax debt, no child support, no judgments, no cosigners, no gambling losses, no businesses within last six years, and no prior bankruptcy cases.

By taking out a reverse mortgage, Mrs. McBride can pay off her existing mortgage, her car, and her credit card debt. In addition, she can receive some additional income or take a lump sum to fix up her home to make it easier for her to live there as she gets older. She can also protect her home from future creditors because she will eliminate the excess equity over and above her homestead exemption of $82,775. Her monthly expenses would decrease, making it easier for her to live on her monthly income.

Documents needed:

- Tax assessment showing valuation of home

- Statements showing balance of home, car, and credit cards

- Credit report

- Recorded deed for her home

Factors considered showing why this is the best option:

First, the amount of the debt is such that she has to do something.

Second, the type of debt includes secured items with a lot of equity that creditors could attempt to seize if nothing is done.

Third, although her income is steady, it has decreased, so her ability to pay creditors is at risk.

Fourth, because she would lose her assets, including her home and vehicle, a Chapter 7 bankruptcy is not the correct choice. Since she cannot discharge the debt through bankruptcy, she needs a way to pay her debt, but she doesn't have the income to support all the payments she needs to make as it now stands.

Fifth, although her income is protected from creditors (i.e., Social Security income and retirement benefits), her assets are not protected. She has too much equity; she can protect only $82,775 of equity in her home, and she has over $150,000 of equity in it ($175,000 value minus $25,000 mortgage). She also can protect only $4,425 of equity in her car, but she has over $8,000 in it ($13,000 value minus $5,000 owed). A reverse mortgage would pay off all her creditors and reduce the amount of equity in her home to protect it from future creditors.

Sixth, her income would stay basically constant. She needs to reduce her expenses so she can manage her anticipated expenses. A reverse mortgage would allow her to reduce her expenses substantially and allow her to retain her assets.

I have had cases in which a retired couple had tens of thousands of dollars of unsecured debt such as credit card debt and has substantial (but not too much) equity in a home. Since their income is protected from creditors, they might choose not to file bankruptcy. However, since they want to preserve their homes for the benefit of their children, they file bankruptcy so their children, not the credit card companies, receive the equity in their homes. In fact, since the benefit is more for grown sons and daughters than for their parents, it's not uncommon for the sons and daughters to pay the bankruptcy costs for their parents.

In this case, if the credit card debt was incurred prior to Mr. McBride's death and was more substantial, and assuming the car and the house were jointly owned, if the McBrides had filed Chapter 7 bankruptcy while he was still alive, the equity in their home and their vehicle would have been fully protected in bankruptcy and they would have received a discharge of all their unsecured debt. Frankly, it is important for couples in retirement to consider the cash flow situation of the survivor and make plans to protect the assets for the benefit of the surviving spouse.

Sometimes we will file a bankruptcy, get rid of judgment liens, and advise a client to get a reverse mortgage to reduce expenses and increase cash flow. Sometimes we will recommend a client get a reverse mortgage first, make any repairs to the house, and pay any non-dischargeable debts such as student loans (cosigned loans to grandchildren) or taxes, and thereafter file a Chapter 7 bankruptcy when we can protect their equity.

Creditor Call Relief Program Strategy

Case History: Joann Maxwell

Joann Maxwell was diagnosed with MS several years ago and finally had to stop working five years ago. She is on Social Security Disability and receives about $1,200/month. She rents and has no valuable assets. To her surprise, she received several

credit cards even though she fully disclosed her condition and income. She used the cards for gifts for family members and for other things she needed and wanted. Of course, the only way she could make the payments was to use one card to pay another, and she's maxed out her cards and owes about $10,000. Collection agencies are starting to call her, and it is very stressful because she has no way to pay them.

Summary of Financial Case:

Single

Social Security Disability income: $14,400/year

No dependents

Rents

No valuable assets or vehicles

Four credit cards: balance $10,000

No student loans, no tax debt, no child support, no judgments, no cosigners, no gambling losses, no businesses within the last six years, and no prior bankruptcies.

Joann is considered "judgment proof" in that she has no assets creditors can take and no income they can garnish. It does not make economic sense for her to file a bankruptcy, and she could not afford to do so any way.

A few law firms throughout the country are offering a program in which they take collection agencies' calls on behalf of their clients. Our firm calls our program "The Creditor Call Relief Program." Under the Fair Debt Collection Practices Act (FDCPA), collection agencies must stop calling a debtor if the debtor instructs the collection agency in writing to stop communicating with the debtor. Our program sends letters to the collection agencies informing them to stop calling the client/debtor and call our firm instead. The client/debtor monitors and keeps notes of any potential violations of the FDCPA. If a collection agency continues to call the client/debtor after proper notification, the client/debtor can sue the collection agency for violation of the FDCPA and recover $1,000 statutory damages, actual damages, and attorneys' fees. Although there is a potential benefit to suing a collection agency, the major benefit is stopping harassing calls.

It is important to realize that this program doesn't discharge debt; creditors can still sue and obtain a judgment. The program is like taking medicine to help with the pain (of harassing calls) but doesn't cure the underlying problem, (the debt). However, as noted above, Joann is judgment proof anyway.

In deciding whether this program makes sense, we first consider the fact that the amount of debt is on the low end—only $10,000—but is relatively high in relation to Joann's income—$14,000/year. A Chapter 7 bankruptcy would be the best solution to get rid of the debt, but she cannot realistically afford it.

Second, the type of debt (unsecured) could clearly be discharged in a bankruptcy, but again, the problem is her inability to afford a bankruptcy.

Third, the amount and type of income makes it less economically sensible to file bankruptcy. Joann's Social Security Disability income is protected from creditor garnishment. Regular Social Security, retirement, unemployment income, worker compensation, and any other disability income are also protected from garnishments. Also, because of her low income, she could not afford to pay the fees to file a bankruptcy.

Fourth, her living expenses are covered by her Social Security Disability income, but she has no way to pay her credit card debt.

Fifth, Joann does not have assets creditors could take or encumber. This is part of the reason she is "judgment proof."

Sixth and finally, her financial future does not look as though it will change.

Again, different facts would suggest a different outcome. For example, if Joann owned a home with a significant amount of equity, we would recommend she try to file a bankruptcy. This would not be for her benefit but rather for her adult children, and we would suggest the adult children pay for the bankruptcy since they will benefit from it. Also, if Joann's condition was such that it would improve and allow her to support herself again, she would want to file a bankruptcy once she returned to full-time employment.

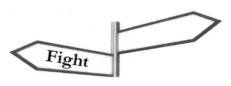

Fighting Creditors

Sometimes individuals and couples find themselves in situations in which they are temporarily in a negative cash flow situation and cannot meet even their basic living expenses and are being pursued by creditors for debt they cannot pay. Because of the negative cash flow, they should not file bankruptcy since they could easily incur more debt after filing and then would not be able to refile bankruptcy for another eight years. Furthermore, if they cannot cover their basic living expenses, they cannot afford the cost of a bankruptcy. They still need to plan to file bankruptcy, but they need to stall creditors until they have positive cash flow again. This is the time to consider fighting creditors. Many debtors in negative cash flow situations will actually do the opposite—they will ignore creditors by not opening their mail, not answering the phone, and ignoring pending lawsuits.

The big secret creditors do not want you to know is that they are hoping you will ignore pending lawsuits because it is expensive for the creditors to prove you owe them money, and many times the creditors have destroyed the documentation to prove you owe them.

When you decide to fight creditors, you need to stay in contact with them. Tell them you don't have sufficient cash flow to pay them. You don't have to talk with them every time they call, but you should talk with them at least once a month. Never lie to a creditor or a collection agency; they will use that against you in future calls. Make sure to let them know you will speak with them once a month (not several times a day) to update them on your situation and ask them not to call more (don't expect them, however, to comply with this request). If they send you a letter demanding payment, it will often include language required by the FDCPA in which they give you thirty days to dispute their claim. Again, with this strategy of fighting creditors, you always want to dispute the debt, and you should do so in a letter sent certified, return receipt requested. Keep track of all your contacts with creditors and who said what. Be aware—they are keeping track of all the contacts they have with you. Having a diary by your phone to record the details of the call is ideal.

The reason why you want to keep in contact with your creditors is that it will delay their pursuit of a lawsuit. Also, if you might possibly need to pay off the creditor in the future, you want to prevent, if possible, the added expenses of attorneys' fees.

If you are served with a summons and complaint, you want to make sure you "answer" it. The "answer" must be in writing; you must sign the answer, and a copy must be sent to the attorneys for the plaintiff (the creditor), and the clerk of the court where the action is brought. The court to which the lawsuit has been brought is listed on the top left-hand corner of the summons and complaint. Usually, the court clerk's address is not listed in the paperwork, so you will need to look that up on the Internet or in the blue pages of the phone book. The creditor's attorney's address is usually at the end of the summons and complaint on the right side.

You could raise several defenses to dispute the claim in the lawsuit. One defense is to deny you owe the amount they're requesting in the complaint. You may think you owe them less or even more than they're asking. If they are asking for interest, late fees, and/or attorneys' fees and you dispute the amount, they must show a written contract that entitles them to those fees. If you made some payments, they need to provide a full accounting of charges and payments.

Other potential defenses include:

- Improper jurisdiction—basically, an assertion that they brought a lawsuit in a jurisdiction (place) where you don't live or haven't lived.

- Expiration of statute of limitations—the deadline to bring a lawsuit has expired because creditors have only six years from the date you incurred the loan, or paid on the loan, or acknowledged the loan to file suit, whichever occurs later. (This is why you never want to admit you owe the debt).

- Identity theft—you didn't personally incur the debt; your identity was stolen by a third party that incurred the debt without your consent.

- Latches—the creditor has taken so long to pursue the claim that you no longer have the evidence to prove you don't owe the debt.

Keep in mind that you need to have a basis to raise a defense; you can be fined if you claim a defense but know you have no basis for doing so.

If you owe the debt, your likelihood of successfully fighting creditors is very small. If a collection agency is suing you, the likelihood of successfully defeating the collection agency increases because it would need to pay the original creditor for the evidence that you owe the debt, and so it may choose not to pursue the claim against you if you "answer" the complaint in writing and file it with the court. As well, the collection agency may not be able to get the evidence because the original creditor may have destroyed the evidence. At least you can delay the collection in the hopes that you can improve your cash flow and make filing a Chapter 7 bankruptcy a better option.

You may not want to pursue this option of fighting creditors in the event you have assets the creditor could go after, or if when you return to work, you'll make "too much" money to file a Chapter 7. The reason is that the creditor pursuing the action can often add attorneys' fees, and you could end up making the bill much larger.

Case History: Michael Richardson

Michael is single, unemployed, and receiving unemployment benefits. He hopes to find another job soon, but it has been several months since he lost his job due to downsizing. When he was working, he made about $40,000/year. Michael's unemployment is sufficient to cover his basic expenses, but he no longer has health insurance and has incurred some medical expenses he cannot pay.

He has also been using credit cards to help pay for emergencies such as car repairs. One of his old debts is in the hands of a collection agency that has served him with a summons and complaint lawsuit. Michael decides to fight the summons and complaint and submits a written answer denying he owes the amount the collection agency claims he owes.

Summary of Financial Case:

  Single

  Income: $18,000/year (unemployment benefits)

  Tax refund: nominal

  No dependents

  2001 Chevy Malibu: paid for, value $1,500

  Six credit cards: $21,000

  Two medical bills: $2,000

  Total unsecured debt: $23,000

No student loans, no tax debt, no child support, no judgments, no cosigners, no gambling losses, no businesses within last six years, and no prior bankruptcy cases.

Fighting his creditors is an excellent strategy for Michael since he doesn't have the money to pay the creditors, he cannot afford a bankruptcy at this time, he has the potential to incur additional debt because of the lack of health insurance, and even if he loses the lawsuit, his unemployment cannot be garnished. Finally, he has no available assets for the creditors to take. When Michael gets a job again, he will likely make the same or less as he earned previously, so he will not make "too much" to file a Chapter 7 when he can get health insurance again.

Many find themselves in situations similar to Michael's, which explains why bankruptcy filings go down when the economy suffers with high unemployment and why bankruptcy filings increase when the economy improves and individuals get jobs again. Although it seems counterintuitive that the number of bankruptcies decreases when the economy declines, when viewed from this perspective, it becomes more understandable.

Documents needed for fighting creditors:

- Payoff statements for all bills

- All credit card, medical, and loan bills

- All collection letters

- All lawsuits

- Proof of payments/receipts of purchase

- Credit report

- All correspondence with creditors

- Diary of all contact with creditors

Factors why fighting creditors is the right choice for Michael:

First, Michael cannot pay off his debt in a reasonable amount of time even with a job.

Second, the type of debt is unsecured; thus, it can ultimately be discharged in bankruptcy. It is always better to avoid a judgment, as it will remain on your credit report even after a bankruptcy and even after the judgment has been paid, although it will show as being "satisfied." A judgment is more damaging to your credit report than is a bankruptcy. With a bankruptcy, you can get credit, but with a collectable judgment, it is nearly impossible to get credit.

Third, Michael's income is low but hopefully will increase soon. Because of this insufficient income, it's not the best time for

Michael to file bankruptcy because he will potentially still be acquiring debt.

Fourth, as noted above, Michael's expenses exceed, on occasion, his income. He needs all his income for survival.

Fifth, Michael's assets are such that they would be protected from creditors in a lawsuit or in bankruptcy.

Sixth, Michael's history indicates that he can return to a job with pay sufficient to cover all his expenses, but at this time, he's not there. In addition, he will most likely still qualify for a Chapter 7 bankruptcy when he does get a job.

If Michael owned some assets that creditors could take if a lawsuit is successful, it might make more sense to sell those assets to pay for his medical expenses. Unlike credit card companies that can spread risk of loss over millions of people, medical providers cannot, and so he would want to avoid creating issues with those he may need in the future to help with medical problems.

If Michael ultimately gets a very good job and makes "too much" to file bankruptcy later, he may want to do whatever he can now, including getting help from family or friends, to file a bankruptcy while he is still unemployed rather than trying to fight the creditors. Otherwise, he may just end up owing much more than he does now with all the extra attorneys' fees and costs.

OPTIONS TO AVOID IF POSSIBLE

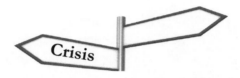

Robbing Peter to Pay Paul - Crisis Management

The first and biggest mistake people in debt make is reacting in a crisis management mode. In reality, this method of dealing with debt is no strategy at all. Credit card companies call repeatedly, demanding immediate payment, and taking these calls frustrates, embarrasses, and stresses the debtor. They react by paying a credit card debt with money that should have gone to a car or house payment; this is classic robbing Peter to pay Paul. Having paid their credit card debt, they now have jeopardized their homes and their cars.

They need to step back and decide on their priorities. For most people in debt, cars are critical; that's what gets them to work. Studies show that Americans, forced to choose between paying mortgages or making car payments, will make the car payments. The second priority, if the house payment is cheaper or at least not more than renting, is making house payments.

Anyone in this situation needs to create a plan, because creditors have a plan. Those in debt need to figure out how much money they have coming in each month and what expenditures they need to survive. In other words, they have to create a real strategy. If their budgets and plans show no money for making credit card payments, it may be time for them to consider a bankruptcy. Trying to use crisis management and robbing Peter to pay Paul has a zero chance of success.

Case Study: Vanessa Westerly

Vanessa, a single mom, had a difficult month. Her car needed $400 in repairs, and her daughter broke her arm in a bicycle accident when they were visiting Vanessa's sister out of their area. The medical insurance deductible was higher because they couldn't use an "in network" doctor and because they used the emergency room. Things were slowing at work, so not only did she not get any overtime, she didn't get to work full forty-hour weeks. When the cable bill came due, Vanessa couldn't pay it.

Summary of Financial Case:

Divorced

Income: $30,000/year, $40,000/year with overtime

Child support: $6,000

Tax refund: $2,500

One dependent

2011 Nissan Sentra: balance $3,000, value $7,500, $250/month payment

Medical bills: $500 for daughter's broken arm

No student loans, no tax debt, no child support, no judgments, no cosigners, no gambling losses, no businesses within the last six years, and no prior bankruptcies.

This situation was a real wake-up call for Vanessa. She was very proud of the fact that she could manage well as a single mother, but she was distressed that she couldn't pay her normal bills and was now in debt with medical bills. Fortunately, the overtime work resumed, and she would be able to pay off the medical debt quickly and resume making her normal monthly bills.

However, she realized she should plan for "emergencies." Vanessa completed a budget; she could live on her regular income and so decided to start a "rainy day" account with her overtime pay and child support. Once she had some savings in the bank, she felt a great deal of peace and pleasure knowing she would not likely be caught in any future dire financial situations.

When a crisis hits, you do what you need to do to get through it, but it's important to ultimately step back and ask, "What can I do to prevent this crisis from happening next time?" Vanessa was smart and did this analysis on her own financial situation. We all have permission to make mistakes when crises hit, but we should learn from those mistakes, do what we can to keep from making them again, and become better prepared for crises. Of course, we're better off if we can learn from the mistakes of others, which is what I hope you will do with this book.

Documents needed to prepare for these types of "emergencies":

- Pay stubs and other income information

- All bills and expenses

- Credit report

- A budget

- Savings

Factors why crisis management was the best option for Vanessa:

First, the amount of her debt was relatively small and could easily be addressed in a few months. This is one of the most important factors.

Second, the type of debt was such that it could be paid in the future with reasonable monthly payments.

Third, her income was normally steady, but she learned it might not always be that way.

Fourth, she could normally cover her expenses with her income; the bad financial month she went through was not typical.

Fifth, her main asset, her car, needed to be in working condition for her to get to work, so she needed to keep it running.

Sixth, her future income looked steady and sufficient, but it was important for Vanessa to realize that the future is always unpredictable, so it was important to be better prepared for the future.

If this hadn't been the first time this had happened, the crisis management strategy wouldn't have been the best strategy. It's okay if it teaches you a lesson, but repeated use of the crisis strategy and using Peter's money to pay Paul is a recipe for disaster. Furthermore, if the amounts are larger, it's important to step back and create a long-term plan.

Gambling

As is the case with crisis management, gambling is no strategy. Usually, people using this technique are in denial of their situation; they gamble as a means of escape from the issues they need to deal with, or their debt is so overwhelming that they cannot see how they could pay it off and will not consider bankruptcy or qualify for it. Gambling, by definition, will never work; it will simply cause more debt or deplete precious resources and assets. Even in the very rare situations in which certain people "win" enough to pay off their current debts, they'll find themselves back in debt in no time unless they change their habits and thinking.

Unfortunately, most poor people believe that gambling is their only chance to get ahead, so they waste their money on lottery tickets and casinos. The other major problem with gambling is that their "wins" are the results of others' losses; they know how difficult it is to suffer, so why would they help create a situation that causes others to suffer?

Case History: Thomas and Monica Stevens

Thomas works for a manufacturing plant as a computer programmer, and Monica is currently an unemployed math teacher. They have two children, ages six and eight. Their home is worth $125,000, they owe about $115,000 on it, and they are current on house payments. They have a 2013 Kia Sedona on which they owe $18,000 and are current, and a 2008 Dodge Charger, which they own outright.

When Monica lost her job, the Stevenses didn't cut back on expenses because they didn't think it would take long for Monica to get another job. Before they knew it, however, they had accumulated $5,000 in credit card debt. When it became clear that Monica would get only substitute teaching jobs on occasion, they reworked their budget so they could live on

Thomas's salary. Since Monica cannot get a job, she has decided to gamble—no, not by playing online poker or going to the racetrack and wasting money the family could not afford, but by gambling with her ability to tutor children in math. This is a form of gambling that some clients can actually profit from. She expects to work after school four days week, for about three hours a day. The goal is to make enough to pay off their credit cards in twelve months.

Summary of Financial Case:

Married

Husband's income: $50,000/year

Wife's income: $10,000/year (estimate)

Total yearly income: $60,000 (estimate)

Tax refunds: $2,500/year

Two dependents

2013 Kia Sedona: balance $18,000, value $17,000, $400/month payments

2008 Dodge Charger: paid for, value $4,000

Two credit cards: $5,000

Total unsecured debt: $5,000

No student loans, no tax debt, no child support, no judgments, no cosigners, no gambling losses, no businesses within the last six years, and no prior bankruptcies.

Monica is going to gamble not with money but on herself and her abilities to help others and create a job for herself. Starting a business is always a gamble, but sometimes it's the best option available. Monica has decided to do something she loves to do—teaching children math. Because of the high need for these services, she can charge $25/hour and should make about $200/week, and she will substitute teach when she's called. So, with making $1,000/month during the school year, the Stevenses are able to pay off the $5,000 in debt and start to save some of her income for other potential needs.

Documents needed:

- All credit card, medical, and other loan bills

- Credit report

- Budget

- Analysis of skills, talents, and interests for potential business opportunities

- Analysis of potential need for your services and estimated income

- A plan for implementing the business

Factors why this is the best option:

First, the amount of debt can be reasonably paid within a short time.

Second, the secured debt—the car and house payments—can be covered by Thomas's income. Once the credit cards are paid off, they can save some of Monica's income. The total debt is not sufficient to consider filing bankruptcy.

Third, Thomas's income is sufficient and steady to pay the necessary expenses, and Monica's income, while less than her potential, will be enough to pay off the credit cards.

Fourth, their expenses are stable and can be covered by Thomas's income.

Fifth, their assets are such that they are protected from creditors, but Thomas's income could be garnished if the credit card creditors got a judgment.

Sixth, their income is likely to go up in the future, and Monica's tutoring will allow them to get out of debt and save money. Furthermore, this plan provides a lot of flexibility if the Stevenses decided they want to have another child, for example.

If their credit card and unsecured debt were substantially higher, I would suggest the Stevenses consider a Chapter 7 bankruptcy.

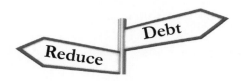

Debt-Reduction Strategy

A debt-reduction strategy may work only 10 percent of the time, and it can leave someone in a worse situation than doing nothing.

Case History: Ronald and Nancy Hall

Ronald's business can make him a lot of money quickly, but it's extremely inconsistent and variable. Nancy is a retail clerk at a clothing store. She doesn't make a lot, but it's enough to pay household expenses, including rent, utilities, food, gas, and car insurance. She also has health insurance for the family.

Because of the variable nature of Ronald's income, he used credit cards to buy the tools and technology he needed to get his business started and pay for emergencies, such as repairs to the cars or trips to help his elderly parents in another state. Business has not been very good lately, and he now has about $23,000 in credit card debt. Though the business is seasonal, it will not be too long before things pick up, and he loves the work. At the moment, there is no income to pay the credit card companies, which are calling several times a day.

Summary of Financial Case:

Married

Husband's income: $30,000–$60,000/year, made mostly during the summer and extremely variable

Wife's income: $22,000/year

Total income: $52,000–$82,000/year

One dependent

Rent

2002 Chevy Prizm: paid for, value $1,000

2002 Ford F-150 Truck: paid for, value $3,000

Business and business assets: $15,000

Three credit cards, all in Ronald's name: $23,000

No student loans, no tax debt, no child support obligations, no judgments, no cosigners, no gambling losses, and no prior bankruptcies.

Although debt-reduction programs work as often as winning the lottery, it's probably an option Ron should try.

Documents needed:

- Bills from secured creditors showing the amount needed to pay off the loans
- All credit card, medical, and other bills
- Credit report
- Budget

Factors why this option is the best for the Halls:

First, while Ron has enough debt to justify filing a Chapter 7, he will be required to shut down his business and would risk losing his business assets in the bankruptcy process. The fact that Ron has only three creditors increases the chance he can work something out with them. If Ron had over a dozen creditors, it would be essentially impossible for him to resolve his debt in this manner. The truth is that most creditors will not even respond to your requests for settlement.

Second, the type of debt would qualify for a bankruptcy but for reasons stated above, it is not the best option.

Third, Ron could file a Chapter 13, protect his assets, and keep his business going, but he would need to make regular monthly payments, and his income is not steady enough for this plan. He'd have to have a large amount of money to offer creditors to try the debt-reduction method. A creditor accepting a reduction in the amount owed will not accept payments but will accept a reduction because money now is worth more than a promise of payment in the future. Also, debt owed to a creditor willing to accept a reduction must be significantly in default. The default must put the creditor on the verge of bringing legal action for payment; the debt must be six months to a year behind or more. The creditor must have tried every other method to collect and must believe the debt is essentially uncollectable.

In Ron's case, when he makes money, it's in a large amount at once, so he could possibly have the amount needed to offer a creditor. He should wait until he has the money before he starts negotiations and makes an offer. He should offer less than he could actually pay so he can increase his offer; he should never make an offer or agreement he cannot fulfill.

Ron has to make sure that any agreement to settle is in writing because once any funds are paid, creditors will nearly always claim there was no agreement to settle. Ron also needs to be aware that if he settles a $12,000 debt for $7,000, the creditor will send him a 1099 IRS form for $5,000 of debt the creditor "wrote off," and Ron will need to pay income taxes on the $5,000 of forgiven debt.

Fourth, the expenses are such that Nancy can cover the normal monthly expenses and allow Ron's income to be used for debt repayment.

Fifth, given the value of his business and business assets, in a Chapter 13, he would need to pay back all or nearly all his creditors in full. As stated above, in a Chapter 7, Ron would risk losing his business assets, so that's not the best option either.

Sixth, the financial future outlook is that Ron could make a significant amount to make the offers and pay back most of the debt.

Although most debt-reduction plans never work, Ron doesn't have much to lose by trying. However, Ron should put aside the money until he can pay the debt in full or until the creditors settle for less.

Studies show the success rate for this type of strategy is less than 10 percent. Most of the time, those using this strategy find themselves in worse situations than when they started. The time to use this strategy is when you can't file bankruptcy, you have no other option, and you will ultimately be required to pay back the creditors anyway.

Also, do not use debt-reduction companies. You've heard and seen the commercials—"Reduce the amount of your debt to just a fraction of what you owe—pay just 30 to 50 percent of the balance!" The actual success rate of this strategy is about the same as playing the lottery. Only a very small number of creditors are willing to negotiate with debtors. In fact, most creditors will actually become more aggressive in pursuing lawsuits against anyone using these debt-reduction companies. The credit card companies know when you need to file bankruptcy by looking at your credit report. If you choose not to file bankruptcy when you should, the credit card companies assume you cannot do so; they think you have more income than they thought or that you have valuable assets that cannot be protected in bankruptcy. The credit card companies also want to send a strong message that they are not interested in debt-settlement offers.

A few credit card companies are willing to settle with consumers, but the consumers must be in serious default on their payments (enough to destroy their credit scores), and the consumers would need the entire amount of any settlement to be paid in one payment (i.e., no payment plans).

Keep in mind that if you successfully negotiate and pay a reduction, the credit card company will notify the IRS of the amount it "wrote off," and the IRS will consider the "saved" amount income on which you will have to pay income taxes. In bankruptcy, you don't have to worry about this.

We've tried negotiating debt-settlement agreements for clients, but we've found that it's impossible to provide the service for a price those in debt can afford; to do it correctly could cost $3,000 to $7,000 or more, and that's just the attorneys' fees, not the settlement amount for the creditor. As well, many creditors refuse to settle and will simply file a lawsuit. Since usually the total cost of filing bankruptcy is less than $2,000 and you don't have to pay back creditors, we find filing bankruptcy is a better solution.

The problem with debt settlement is that you cannot force creditors to accept your proposals. What typically happens with a debt-settlement company is that it has you pay them as much as they think they can get from you, upfront and in monthly payments, and then it tells you to stop paying your creditors because as long as you're paying the creditors, the creditors won't settle. Once you're sufficiently behind and creditors have added interest, late fees, and over-the-limit fees, the debt-settlement company (which frequently has a deal with some creditors to settle for a percentage of the total debt) will push for you to pay what you owed when you started the program. So, it makes it look as though its system works. However, many creditors will never settle; they will sue you for what you owe plus all the extras and attorneys' fees. Any judgment they win could become a lien on your home or will result in a garnishment of your wages.

In sum, clients using debt-settlement companies end up paying a lot of money to these companies and end up with judgments against them anyway. The debt settlement companies don't tell you the full story, and they use your fear of bankruptcy to get you to sign up for their supposed services.

Again, if you do settle, the amount the creditors write off then becomes income on which you'll have to pay income tax. The creditors will send you a 1099 at the end of the year disclosing to the IRS the amount they wrote off. I can't tell you how many clients have told this same story.

We're willing to act as coaches if you want to hire us to try this method. We won't negotiate for you because we know this doesn't work, and we don't want you to be disappointed in us when the attempts to settle just make your financial situation worse.

Borrowing from Relatives

If you want a great way to destroy family relationships, borrow money from relatives. Because of the family relationship, such loans usually don't have legal documents covering repayment obligations or what happens in the case of default, and so on. Very often, the lending relative considers the money a loan, but the borrower believes it's a gift that should be but doesn't have to be repaid. Borrowers think the loan can be repaid when it's convenient, but the relatives doing the lending, if they borrowed the money from traditional resources, must pay it back on a set schedule. When the borrower takes a vacation or buys an expensive item, what's the lending relative going to think?

Creditors can't look to your relatives to pay your debt. Why get your relatives involved in your financial mess? One of the best things about bankruptcy is that the cost of getting legal help to file a bankruptcy is very low, and most lawyers have payment plans, making it possible for you to get the help you need without asking your relatives for help.

Furthermore, paying back relatives right before filing bankruptcy can create a huge problem for you and your relatives. Traditional creditors have convinced Congress that it's unfair for a debtor to repay a relative right before filing bankruptcy. Congress has passed a law that requires debtors to disclose if they've paid back relatives in the twelve months prior to filing bankruptcy, giving the relatives preference, so to speak, and requires the trustee to sue the relatives for a return of the money so it can be distributed to all creditors proportionately.

Some clients have the mistaken belief that when they file bankruptcy, they cannot repay their creditors after the bankruptcy is over, including relatives. This is not the case. Anyone who files a bankruptcy can always repay creditors; bankruptcy just prevents creditors from trying to collect the debt. So if you owe relatives money, don't pay them prior to filing bankruptcy, but let them know in advance of your need to file bankruptcy, and let them know you'll pay them back and that your filing bankruptcy makes it easier for you to pay them back.

Furthermore, in the event you can't pay them back, it may be possible for your relatives to deduct the loan loss from their income taxes. The lending relative should consult a tax professional on this issue.

Finally, it's important to list the lending relative on your bankruptcy petition. For one reason, bankruptcy law requires you to list all creditors, and you might be denied a discharge from your debts for failing to do so. In addition, it's possible there could be assets in your bankruptcy case, and then you'll want to make sure your relative can recover some of the claim.

If you borrow from relatives to solve your financial crisis, you'll probably destroy or seriously negatively affect your relationship with them, and it will most likely not fix your economic problems.

Case History: Bruce and Cindy Jensen

The Jensens owned a small business six years ago but weren't that knowledgeable about the legalities of how to run it. When New York State caught up with the Jensens, they were forced to

close their business, and they ended up owing $8,000 in unpaid sales taxes, penalties, and fees.

Five years later, the amount of that tax debt with interest is now over $12,000. The Jensens work full time, rent, and have only a couple of old cars. They have no retirement accounts. New York State is now threatening to garnish their wages. The Jensens found an attorney who could actually communicate with New York State taxing authorities, and this is extremely difficult, since New York State relies primarily on computers for its collection process. The Jensen's attorney has been able to get New York State to agree to a settlement of $5,000 to resolve the tax debt. The attorney tells them it's unusual to get such an offer and they should do whatever they can to complete the settlement. Bruce's brother Mark is willing to loan Bruce the money, and the brothers agree in writing that Bruce will make payments of $235/month for two years and will pay Mark 12 % (percent) interest.

Summary of Financial Case:

Married

Husband's income: $21,000/year

Wife's income: $15,000/year

Total income: $36,000/year

Tax refunds: nominal

No dependents

2000 Nissan Sentra: paid for, value $1,000

2003 Kia Spectra: paid for, value $1,000

No credit cards, medical bills, or personal loans

Tax debt: $12,000, negotiated to $5,000

No student loans, no child support, no judgments, no cosigners, no gambling losses, and no prior bankruptcies.

Since the Jensens cannot file bankruptcy to resolve their debt to New York State and they have no other resources, it makes sense in this particular case to borrow the money. In fact, it's only by borrowing money from relatives or a third party that it's possible to settle like this with the government on taxes. In addition, it's important that the terms of the agreement between the brothers be spelled out and agreed upon to minimize misunderstandings in the future.

Documents needed to pursue this option (the list of documents New York State needs is provided later in the discussion regarding taxes. Below is a list of documents Mark, the brother, should review):

- Offer to settle by New York State Department of Taxation and Finance

- Credit report

- Pay stubs of Bruce and Cindy

Factors why borrowing from a relative is the best option:

First, the amount of the original debt is sufficient to file bankruptcy, especially given the Jensen's income, but this is not the deciding factor.

Second, since the type of debt is sales taxes, this is not dischargeable in a bankruptcy, and so bankruptcy is not the best option.

Third, although the Jensen's income is steady, it's very modest. They can afford reasonable payments but not for a significant period.

Fourth, the Jensen's expenses are modest, especially since they own their vehicles outright, but given the age of the vehicles, it's likely they will need significant repairs or need to be replaced in the future, so a short repayment period is best.

Fifth, since the Jensens have no valuable assets other than their vehicles, which they need for work, they're able to get a settlement as they did with New York State. However, they have no real resources to pay the settlement offer, so they must look to relatives for help.

Sixth, the Jensens have stabilized their income, but because of the tax debt they acquired, they cannot get ahead until it's paid. Once the debt to Mark is repaid, the Jensens can start to get ahead.

If the tax debt was instead medical bills, credit cards, or business vendors, bankruptcy would have been a better choice.

Consolidating Debt

Consolidating debt does not get rid of debt; it just changes to whom it's owed. The big problem with this technique is that when people use consolidation loans to pay off their credit cards, they start using their credit cards again and the debt problem explodes. People claim they will not do so, but emergencies happen, and they turn to their credit cards again if they are their only sources for funds. Those who take out consolidation loans need to make sure the interest rate is lower than the current rate or otherwise they'll simply be paying more back.

Case History: George and Mimi Stack

George and Mimi had a difficult couple of years; Mimi got ill, and the doctors couldn't figure out her problem. Although they had health insurance, they had to use a variety of doctors, some of whom were out of their network, and some of whom were practitioners of alternative medicine not covered by their insurance. The deductibles and uncovered expenses started to add up, and the Stacks owe about twenty-three doctors, clinics, and labs a total of $7,200. Some of these amounts owed are as low as $220, but one is $1,200.

Fortunately, a doctor was able to figure out Mimi's medical problem and resolve it, but all the medical providers want their money now, which the Stacks cannot afford to pay. One of the clinics is threatening to sue, and some providers are charging 18 percent interest.

The Stacks have arranged for a consolidated loan from their credit union at 6 percent interest with payments of $320/month over twenty-four months. The Stacks are young and have not yet started a family; they make fairly good incomes, but Mimi has not been able to work because of her illness. She plans to return to work now that her medical problem has been resolved. They have two older cars they bought from their parents for a reasonable price. They still are renting. Fortunately, they don't have any student loans or credit card debt.

Summary of Financial Case:

Married

Husband's income: $35,000/year

Wife's income: $27,500/year (when working)

Total yearly income: $35,000 to $62,500

Tax refunds: nominal

No dependents

2004 Ford Taurus: paid for, value $2,000

2001 Ford Explorer: paid for, value $1,000

Rent

No credit cards or loans

Medical bills: $7,200

Total unsecured debt: $7,200

No student loans, no tax debt, no child support obligations, no judgments, no cosigners, no gambling losses, no businesses in the last six years and no prior bankruptcies

It makes sense for the Stacks to use a consolidated loan in this situation. Their debt is insufficient to justify filing bankruptcy. Because of the large number of creditors (even with the relatively small amounts of each debt), the cash flow they have makes it impossible to pay the various medical providers over the short period of time they're demanding payments. Also, it's better to avoid a judgment because they'd be unable to get any credit, including a consolidation loan. The Stacks also want to be able to protect their credit so they can someday buy a home.

Documents needed to pursue this strategy:

- All medical bills

- Credit report

- Budget

Factors why consolidating the debt is the best option:

First, the amount of the debt is insufficient to consider bankruptcy. However, the high number of individual debts makes it nearly impossible to pay the debts as required by the medical providers.

Second, the type of debt is such that it could be included in a bankruptcy since it is unsecured debt, but as noted above, this is not the deciding factor.

Third, although the Stack's income is sufficient to pay the debt if it could be paid over two years, they couldn't afford to make monthly payments on all the individual debts. A consolidated loan makes reasonable monthly payment amounts possible. Hopefully, Mimi can get a job soon; this would allow them to pay off their consolidated debt even sooner and start saving for a home.

Fourth, the Stack's expenses are not unusual.

Fifth, the Stack's assets would be protected in a bankruptcy, but again, the determining issue is the amount of debt.

Sixth, the Stack's future looks bright; it appears that Mimi's illness is over.

If the amount of their debt were higher, the Stacks might want to consider bankruptcy. Another situation in which consolidation makes sense is with student loans. As will be noted later under the student loan section, generally, the best thing to do is to consolidate all student loans under the Income-Based Repayment (IBR) program in which the repayment amount is based on your income.

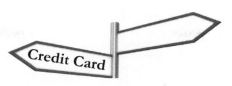

Using One Credit Card to
Pay Another Credit Card

Using one credit card to pay off other credit cards seems to be a favorite strategy to try to avoid bankruptcy. The problem is that if you need to file bankruptcy and you have been using this strategy, the new credit card company may claim you were fraudulent in getting new credit right before filing bankruptcy and may bring a non-dischargeable action against you when you file bankruptcy. It's generally better to leave one creditor unpaid than to get a new creditor involved in the matter.

Furthermore, the debtor frequently goes back to using that first card again, taking on new debt. Most of my clients explain that they were just trying to reduce their interest rates, which may be partially true, but it doesn't stop the second credit card company from claiming fraud.

By using this method, you'll likely need to delay filing your bankruptcy petition if you need to file, and you will need to try to make payments on the new credit card. You could avoid all this by not bringing a new credit card company into the situation in the first place. This is why it's so important to be very honest about your situation. If you're going through a truly temporary financial difficulty or if you can easily make the payments, this could be a strategy to reduce the interest rate and decrease the payment period. However, if your financial problem is not short term, it's better to be honest with yourself and not get more creditors into your financial problem.

Case History: Ronald and Lisa Murphy

The Murphys took out a furniture loan for $8,500 with no interest for two years. The payment was only $100/ month, and they've been paying for nearly two years. However, they realized that they still owed over $6,000 and that the interest rate was going from zero to over 21 percent in another month. At $100/ month, it would take over fifteen years to pay off the balance at that higher interest rate. They thought they could pay it off with their tax refund, but sadly, Congress increased taxes and they'll receive only about $2,000 from the government rather than the $5,000 they used to get.

However, their income and credit is good, and they still receive offers for "no interest" balance transfers from credit card companies. They use their $2,000 tax refund to pay down the debt and use a balance transfer to cover the remaining $4,000. The Murphys read the fine print on the credit card disclosures and realize they will still pay a transfer fee, but it is less than the 21 percent interest rate they'd otherwise be paying. Since they want to get the amount paid in a year while the interest rate is at 0 percent on the balance transfer with the new credit card, they increase the payments to $350. Next time, the Murphys will do the math before getting into another furniture loan.

Summary of Financial Case:

Married

Husband's income: $51,000/year

Wife's income: $33,000/year

Total income: $84,000/year

Tax refunds: $2,000/year

Rent

2007 Dodge Grand Caravan: paid for, value $5,000

2012 Nissan Altima: balance $7,500, value $10,000, $330/month payment

Furniture loan: $6,100

No student loans, no tax debt, no child support, no judgments, no cosigners, no gambling losses, no businesses within the last six years, and no prior bankruptcy cases.

The Murphys got tricked into a furniture loan because they didn't realize the payments in the first two years would not be enough to pay off the loan before the interest rate was to increase substantially. Fortunately, they don't have a lot of debt and they have excellent income and credit. They now know better than to get into that situation again. Since they now know what they need to get this debt paid off quickly, they can reduce the interest rate and thus have more of their payment going toward the principal.

Documents needed:

- Furniture loan paperwork

- Furniture loan payoff balance

- Credit card offer paperwork, including the fine print

- Tax refund

Factors why transferring the furniture loan balance to a credit card is a viable solution:

First, the amount of the debt is relatively low.

Second, the furniture debt is secured; the furniture could be repossessed, although it is doubtful the furniture company would bother taking back two-year-old furniture.

Third, the Murphy's income is more than sufficient to pay off the loan in a year.

Fourth, the Murphy's expenses recently went down after they paid off one of their car loans, so they can easily make a higher furniture loan payment.

Fifth, the Murphy's assets can be protected in bankruptcy, but this is not the deciding issue for this case.

Sixth, the Murphy's current and future financial situation looks great. In fact, they've learned to be wary of no-interest and low payments. Once this is paid off, the Murphys want to start saving for a home.

Getting a Second Mortgage

In Upstate New York, you can protect $82,775 equity for you and $82,775 equity for your spouse in your house, assuming the home is jointly owned, from creditors. For example, if your jointly owned home is worth $200,000 and you have a $34,450 mortgage, you can protect all your $165,550 equity from creditors in or out of bankruptcy. New York State has decided you should be able to make sure you can retain your home even if you owe credit cards and you have a judgment against you. Don't, however, make the mistake of getting a second mortgage and jeopardizing your home in the process.

Getting a second mortgage is rarely ever a good way to pay off debt. Why convert unsecured, potentially dischargeable credit card debt into secured debt and thereby jeopardize your home? It breaks my heart every time clients lose their homes because they've taken out second mortgages to pay off debt rather than just filing bankruptcy, because they still have to file bankruptcy anyway. Getting a second mortgage has the same problems as getting a consolidated loan in that you're more likely to just charge up the credit cards again.

Case History: Jay and Jackie Lerner

The Lerners' lovely home is worth about $250,000, and they owe only $50,000 on it. Though they're empty nesters, they still have about ten years before they retire. They helped their children with student loans and owe $85,000 in student loan debt. Otherwise, they've been diligent in saving for retirement,

and they have no other unsecured debt. They have two reliable cars, a 2013 Nissan Altima and a 2011 Honda CRV with monthly payments of $485 and $430.

Their children have finished college, and two are living with the parents so they can also work on paying the student loans. The Lerners may sell their home after they retire, but for now, their home is convenient to work and near their friends. A bank is offering a "no-closing cost" second mortgage with a low interest rate of 4 percent, repayable over ten years at $860/month.

Summary of Financial Case:

Married

Husband's income: $55,000/year

Wife's income: $45,000/year

Total income: $100,000/year

Tax refund: nominal

Two older children living with them

Home: worth $250,000, mortgage balance $50,000

2013 Nissan Altima: balance $16,600, value $15,000

2011 Honda CRV: balance $5,200, value $12,000

Student loans: $85,000

No tax debt, no child support obligations, no judgments, no cosigners, no gambling losses, and no prior bankruptcies.

It would probably make sense for the Lerners to consider getting a second mortgage to pay off the student loan debt for several reasons. First, student loan debt is non-dischargeable in bankruptcy. Second, the Lerners make too much to file bankruptcy (they would have to pay back 100 percent, and the payments would be higher). Third, they have too much equity in their home to qualify for a Chapter 7. When they retire in ten years, they'll have paid off both their mortgages.

Documents needed to pursue this course of action:

- All student loan payoffs

- Credit report

- Budget

- Payoff of first mortgage

Factors why taking a second mortgage is the best option for the Lerners:

First, the amount of debt is high, but this is not the deciding factor.

Second, the primary debt problem is student loans, which are non-dischargeable in bankruptcy so will need to be paid one way or another.

Third, their income is relatively high, so the Lerners could file only a Chapter 13 bankruptcy, which would require full payment of the debt.

Fourth, the expenses are not unusual.

Fifth, the Lerners have too much equity in their home, so they would have to pay the creditors anyway.

Sixth, the Lerners are done with the student loan borrowing but have only ten years to finalize their retirement plans.

If they had dischargeable unsecured debt rather than student loans, and the equity and income was not so large, the Lerners should file a Chapter 7 bankruptcy.

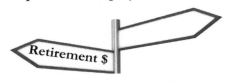

Using Retirement Funds

Using retirement funds is a classic mistake people in debt make all the time. Retirement funds are protected from creditors in or out of bankruptcy. Society realizes it's important for you to save for retirement because the needs you'll have in retirement will be for essentials—food, shelter, and medical care. These future creditors, as I like to call them, who will provide you with these will likely be compelled to do so. They will not have the benefit, as do credit card companies, of considering your credit worthiness and ability to repay when they provide their help and services.

Whom do you think should get the greatest protection, the credit card companies or your future creditors who will provide you with life-sustaining services? I think you'd agree that your future creditors should get your retirement savings. It doesn't matter whether you take a retirement loan or withdraw funds to pay credit cards—both are big mistakes. It's extremely difficult to imagine any time it's better to use retirement funds rather than your current income or file bankruptcy to deal with a debt situation.

Significant tax consequences come with withdrawing funds from an IRA or a 401k. First, there's a 10 percent penalty, so 10 percent of the money is immediately taken by the government. In addition, the money withdrawn is considered income for tax purposes, so it's not uncommon for those who use this approach to find themselves with large tax debts. Essentially, only about half of what's in a retirement account is available for paying down debt. If you're borrowing the money from a 401k, you don't suffer the tax problems, but you do suffer the same problems as those consolidating their debt do.

Furthermore, you lose the potential for compounding interest growth of your retirement.

Case History: Ben and Suzanne Walker

This is a second marriage for Ben and Suzanne. He has three children from his prior marriage who live with his ex-wife, she has two children who live with them, and she receives child support from her ex. Ben and Suzanne both work. After his divorce and prior to his marriage to Suzanne, Ben struggled financially and had gotten behind on his child support payments. Ben's ex was not happy about his failure to stay current on child support and has been pursuing Ben on the matter relentlessly.

Now that Ben has remarried and can share living expenses with Suzanne, he isn't getting further behind with child support but is still behind. Ben's been told he must clear up his arrears or New York State will revoke his driver's license and his electrician's license, both of which he needs. Ben has some retirement funds with the union that he can borrow to catch up his child support.

Summary of Financial Case:

Remarried

Husband's income: $40,000/year (average)

Wife's income: $20,000/year

Wife's child support: $9,600/year

Tax refunds: $3,000/year

Two dependents

2007 Hyundai Elantra: balance $5,500, value $5,000, monthly payments of $350

2008 Dodge Caravan: balance $5,000, value $7,000, monthly payments of $150

Credit card and medical bill debt: $3,000

Back child support: $8,000

No student loans, no tax debt, no cosigners, no gambling losses, and no prior bankruptcies.

Since child support is non-dischargeable in bankruptcy and since Ben is looking at losing his ability to work if his driver's and electrician's licenses are revoked, it makes sense to use his retirement funds to pay off the arrears on his child support.

Documents needed to pursue this option:

- Paperwork/judgment showing the arrears and orders indicating that failure to pay will result in the loss of driver's and electrician's licenses.

- Retirement statement

Factors why using retirement funds is the best option:

First, the amount of the debt is borderline for filing bankruptcy, but this is not the determining factor.

Second, most of the debt is non-dischargeable, and New York State is pursuing an aggressive strategy to get the money now rather than from future wage garnishment; this is the critical reason why it's appropriate to use retirement funds.

Third, the joint income is sufficient for survival and repaying the retirement account.

Fourth, the expenses are now in control with the joint income.

Fifth, although retirement income is protected in bankruptcy, it's his best option for coming up with the money he needs to clear his child support arrears.

Sixth, Ben's future looks stable, the child support arrears are from the past, and it is unlikely Ben will get behind again on child support.

If Ben were not facing immediate loss of his licenses, I'd have suggested he use his current income to pay off the child support arrears.

Working Multiple Jobs

If you're considering taking on another job, first make sure your employer will allow it. Many employers don't approve of their employees working second jobs since they think it will affect their availability and performance on their main jobs. As well, second jobs probably will not pay as well, and their hours will most likely be on nights and weekends. How will working sixty hours a week for, say, seven years affect your family life and your health, both mental and physical?

If you take this approach, be realistic with the numbers. How much will you really have available to pay creditors at the end of the month? How many of your children's events will you miss because of a second job? How will it affect your performance on your regular job? I suggest you do the math and give the matter serious thought to make sure this option makes sense in your case.

Most who consider filing bankruptcy owe in credit card debt about as much as they make a year in income, so let's assume you owe about $30,000 in credit card and medical debt. Let's assume you'll make $10/hour at a second job. You must pay taxes (and you will likely find yourself at a higher tax rate because of the second job's income, so let's assume a 15 percent tax rate. Therefore, your $10/hour is really $8.50/hour.

You'll likely incur additional expenses while you work the second job for takeout or ready-to-eat meals, child care expenses, additional travel expenses, and so on, so let's assume these additional expenses will cost an additional $1/hour; that makes your net income $7.50/hour on the second job. At this rate, with your additional income, it will take 4,000 hours, four years, to pay off the $30,000, and this is assuming you work an additional twenty hours per week for fifty weeks, and it also assumes you're not paying any interest on your debt. If you're paying 15 percent on it, this boosts the repayment period to over six and a half years. If you're paying 19 percent, the repayment period balloons to nine years, figuring payments of $600/month.

Several clients have reported suffering health issues because of the stress of working two jobs, and then they end up filing bankruptcy anyway. One of the biggest problems with working two or more jobs is that it leaves little time for family and other relationships. Children grow up fast, and they need and want a parent there for them. Working a second job may allow you to pay off your debt, but when you're done, will your creditors love you for your sacrifice and effort? Will your children be unhappy and frustrated because you weren't there for them? What's more important, your family or your credit card company?

The number-one filers of bankruptcies are single parents, and I think that's because they realize their family is more important than their creditors.

Case History: Sara Valdez

Sara just got out of graduate school and has a job in her field of study but has student loans totaling $57,000. She's single and twenty-four, and her parents are willing to let her live with

them to keep her expenses down. She continues to drive her old but paid-off car and plans to do so until she pays off her student loans at a rate, she hopes, of $2,000/month. Her first job allows her to pay $1,600 a month, so she decides to work a second job on nights and weekends so she can pay $2,000/month. If she can keep up the payments, she should be able to pay off her loans in two and a half years.

Since Sara is single with no children or other commitments, it's a good time for her to focus on paying off her student loans as quickly as possible. She's keeping her expenses to a minimum to maximize the amount she can pay toward them. With some effort and sacrifice on her part, she can free herself of this debt in a relatively short time.

Summary of Financial Case:

Single

First job: $25,000/year

Second job: $5,000–$10,000/year

Total income: $30,000–$35,000/year

Tax Refund: nominal

No dependents

2000 Honda Civic: paid for, value $1,000

No credit card debt, medical bills, or personal loans

Student loans: $57,000

No tax debt, no back child support, no judgments, no cosigners, no gambling losses, no businesses in the last six years, and no prior bankruptcies.

Since Sara is single and has very few obligations other than her student loans, this is a good time for her to work very hard and pay off her student loan obligations. She's fortunate to have parents who help her minimize her living expenses so she can put most of her money toward her loans.

Documents needed for this course of action:

- Budget
- Student loan bills

Factors why the option is best:

First, the amount of debt is significant, but this is not the deciding factor.

Second, the type of debt is student loans, which cannot be discharged in bankruptcy.

Third, although her income is steady and increasing, she's just starting her career, and so her income is understandably at the lower end of the scale. A second job will increase her income and help get her out of debt in less than three years.

Fourth, she's done a great job of minimizing her expenses so she can focus on paying off the debt quickly.

Fifth, she has no valuable assets she can't otherwise protect.

Sixth, her future looks good, especially if she can sacrifice now and pay off her student loans.

If Sara were working with a governmental or nonprofit entity, she might consider consolidating her loans under the Income-Based Repayment plan (IBR), paying the portion she would need to pay under that program based on her income, and after ten years, her remaining student loans would be forgiven. Obviously, if this were credit card debt, she should file bankruptcy.

Selling Assets

One question we must ask all clients filing bankruptcy is whether they've sold any assets within the previous two years. Sometimes we have had clients try to solve their economic problems by having a yard sale. The problem is that yard sales are a lot of work, and most clients get just a few hundred dollars in the process. Most of their assets—furniture and other personal property—will get them only about ten cents on the dollar; a nice dining room set that cost $1,000 might go for just $100 at a yard sale.

Another type of asset clients often sell is recreational vehicles such as snowmobiles, four-wheelers, or Jet Skis. The problem is that clients are unaware that the store credit card company has a secured lien on these items. If the clients fail to get permission to sell the item and don't turn over the proceeds if they do sell it, the store credit card companies can claim criminal or fraudulent conversion, which means that the client must repay the store credit card for that debt. Had the client not sold the item prior to filing bankruptcy, he or she could have returned the secured item and discharged the debt.

Another popular item frequently sold prior to bankruptcy is jewelry. Again, the pawnshop value of jewelry is ten cents on the dollar; a $1,000 ring will usually get you about $100. The markup on retail jewelry is huge. Because gold and silver are at high prices, you might get a little more than 10 percent, but you'll probably get only about half its value as gold or silver. It's always a good idea to check various places when trying to sell gold or silver, and be careful when trying to sell items on the Internet at places such as Craigslist. There have been several instances where the alleged buyers have simply stolen the items for sale.

However, sometimes the solution to a debt problem is to sell assets.

Case History: Tom and Michelle Jones

The Joneses were very fortunate in that they had bought a home in a great neighborhood before the price of homes started to increase. Tom, who is very handy, upgraded the home with a new kitchen, bathroom, and patio. Michelle is very good with decorating and has created a beautiful home. The house is now worth $250,000, and they owe only about $25,000; they were conscientious about paying down the mortgage and as a result have a great deal of equity in it, but their children are grown, and the house is more than they need.

They have a significant amount in their retirement account, but they took out student loans to get their kids through college that amount to $50,000. Although both make good incomes, they have only about ten years before retirement, and they're paying $555/month toward this debt. The Joneses have decided to downsize and sell their home to pay off the $50,000 of unsecured debt and the $25,000 mortgage, leaving them with nearly $175,000 to buy outright a smaller home.

Summary of Financial Case:

Married

Husband's income: $65,000/year

Wife's income: $35,000/year

Total income: $100,000/year

Tax Refunds: nominal

No dependents

Home: worth $250,000, balance $25,000

2010 Toyota RAV4: paid for, value $7,500

2008 Honda Accord: paid for, value $6,000

No credit card, medical bills, or personal loans

Student loans: $50,000

No tax debt, no child support obligations, no judgments, no cosigners, no gambling losses, and no prior bankruptcies.

Since student loan debt is non-dischargeable and since the Joneses no longer need such a large home, it makes sense to sell the house, pay off the student loans, and purchase outright a new home.

Documents needed to pursue this option:

- Payoff amount for secured debt, especially the house

- Payoff amount for student loans

- Credit report

- Budget

Factors why selling assets may be the best course to take for the Joneses:

First, the amount of the debt is significant and must be repaid.

Second, since the debt is student loans and is non-dischargeable, bankruptcy is not a good option.

Third, the source of income appears steady, but potential health problems for Tom or Michelle could affect their income.

Fourth, the expenses are easily handled by the Joneses' income.

Fifth, another reason for this couple not to consider bankruptcy is that they have too much equity in their home. It is worth $250,000 with only a $25,000 mortgage, so their equity is $225,000, and only $165,550 of equity can be protected in bankruptcy. This leaves a balance of $59,450 to pay unsecured creditors. If the Joneses tried a Chapter 13 plan, their payments would be about $1,100/month for five years.

Sixth, the financial history indicates that the need for future debt is over, but the Joneses need to continue to prepare for retirement.

Payday Loans

Payday loans are the worst type of loan available. Payday loans are not legal in New York, but they're available on the Internet. The amount of payday loans is usually small—a few hundred dollars. The entire goal of payday loan companies is to keep you in debt and paying interest rates that should be illegal, often 700 percent or more, which is the same as borrowing $1 and paying back $8.

The way payday loans usually work is that you write a check to a payday lender in advance (dated two weeks ahead), and the payday lender lends you money now and cashes the check on the due date. If the check bounces, the payday lender will claim it will pursue criminal action (but fortunately most prosecutors won't pursue it). The payday lender will add additional interest and collection fees, making it nearly impossible to pay off the original loan.

In other scenarios, payday lenders will ask for your bank account number to deduct the payment from your checking account. Nearly all our clients who take out payday loans end up having to close their bank accounts because their payday lenders just continue debiting their accounts especially when the borrowers least expect it, and so all their checks bounce.

Be especially aware of Internet payday lenders. One client only applied for a payday loan but several months later got a call claiming the company was going to arrest her for "stealing" money unless she sent money to them by Western Union; this is in spite of the fact that she had never gotten any money from the lender. The lender, however, had her employer's and various relatives' names and numbers, and it threatened to call them about the "stolen" money. Fortunately, she called us before she did anything, and I assured her that what the "lender" was doing was illegal and the "lender" could be arrested if they could be located.

I cannot imagine a situation in which it would make sense to use a payday loan to pay off other debt. Payday loans make no economic sense for the borrower.

Do Nothing

Most people use this method of getting out of debt, but it has only about a 5 percent rate of success in getting people out of debt. It can be a successful strategy for getting out of debt in the right circumstances, but it takes a lot of time to work, and your credit will be bad for a period of time that exceeds the time a bankruptcy could cloud your credit.

What I find sad is that most clients come to me after years of struggling with debt; if they had come in when they first realized their problems, they would have been well on their way to a fresh start. This is one reason we offer a program to help clients improve their credit as quickly as possible.

There's a six-year statute of limitations when it comes to collecting debts which means that creditors have six years to bring a lawsuit to obtain a judgment. The six years begin to run from the last of the following dates: the date of the loan, the last payment made, or the last acknowledgement of the debt (which is why you never want to admit you owe a creditor a debt—always dispute the debt and ask for evidence of the debt).

Case History: Gina Cooper

Gina is a single mother of a nine-month-old and a two-year-old. Her boyfriend, the children's father, has disappeared and was not financially able to provide support for the family in any event. Gina receives government assistance and works part time at a child care facility her children attend while she's working. She barely has enough to take care of herself and her children. A few years ago, she got a couple of credit cards with a limit of $200 each, but because she couldn't make the payments, she now owes over $800 on each.

In addition, she didn't have medical coverage for a few years and owes about $2,100 in medical bills. Finally, she owes a total of $350 to the cable company and for a cell phone her boyfriend got in her name without her permission. She has no assets. She uses the bus to get around. She never finished high school but has been working on getting her GED when she has time.

Summary of Financial Case:

Single

Income: $5,000–10,000/year plus government assistance

Tax refunds: $2,500/year

Two dependents

Credit card debt: $1,600

Medical bills: $2,100

Utility bills: $350

Total unsecured debt: $4,050

No student loans, no tax debt, no child support obligations, no judgments, no cosigners, no gambling losses, and no prior bankruptcies.

Gina doesn't have the resources to pay her debts; she has significant responsibilities with two children. Creditors can try whatever they want, but Gina is "judgment proof," and the creditors will never collect anything from her. She uses her tax refund to pay the arrears she owes to the power company and to buy clothes and supplies for the children. Gina is likely to remain essentially "judgment proof" for a very long time. It's not likely that her creditors will take legal action since the amounts she owes are less than $1,000 each. If she doesn't make payments on any of her debts or admit she owes them, the creditors' ability to sue her to collect will expire six years from the date the debt was incurred or from her last payment. Given her entire situation, it's not likely she will be able, by herself, to change her financial situation in that time. About the time her youngest is in school, Gina's debt will nearly all be uncollectable.

Factors why this option is best:

First, the amount of the debt is small.

Second, the type of debt would be dischargeable in a bankruptcy, but this isn't the determining factor.

Third, Gina's income is very low and not likely to increase any time soon.

Fourth, her expenses consume all her income.

Fifth, she has no assets.

Sixth, the foreseeable future shows little change for the next several years as she focuses her time and energy on her children.

If she had more debt, she'd need to plan to get rid of it in a bankruptcy and could use her tax refund to pay for the cost of filing bankruptcy.

SPECIAL DEBT SITUATIONS

Mortgage Foreclosure/Modification Strategies

In these difficult economic times, many home owners have gotten behind on their mortgages but want to keep their homes. If your income will not support payments even at a lower interest rate, this strategy will not work. The good news is that it takes a minimum of one year to complete a foreclosure after it has started, and it's taking an average of three years to complete a foreclosure in New York State. It's more beneficial for the lender when the owner stays in the property since that minimizes the risk of vandalism.

Getting mortgage lenders to agree to modify mortgages is very difficult because outside of bankruptcy, there's no way to force mortgage lenders to agree to any modifications. Things get really complicated because the entity that lent the money is very often different from the entity that is "servicing" the loan. The entity that lent the money is different from the party that will suffer loss if the home goes into foreclosure. In fact, it's probably the American taxpayer who will likely suffer the loss if a house goes into foreclosure. The "servicer" actually gets more money by foreclosing than it does by making loan modifications. It's important to have a little bit of history of how we got into the mortgage crisis. Overall, there was a disconnect between the party that ultimately takes the risk of failure (which has ended up being the U.S. taxpayer) and the party that agreed to make the loan. What essentially happened is that mortgage brokers who work on commission made more money if the borrower borrowed more and agreed to a more risky type of loan. Mortgage brokers were told they didn't need to verify a person's income or ability to support the mortgage payments. Mortgage brokers could rely on the fact that borrowers stated they made enough money, and they didn't require borrowers to come up with down payments for the houses they bought.

Brokers would hire appraisers to appraise homes, but the appraisers wouldn't get any more work from the brokers unless they appraised the homes for enough to support the mortgages on them, so appraisers had a big incentive to find houses worth what the buyers wanted to pay for them. The mortgage brokers then "sold" these mortgages to a "trust," which meant the mortgage brokers wouldn't take any losses if the loans went bad. The mortgage brokers had huge incentives to make as many loans as they could, "bad" or not.

Many now believe the government and the Federal Reserve (the Fed) did a poor job of regulating the mortgage loan industry. This system inflated the prices of homes because more people could buy homes since they didn't have to put any money down or prove they could afford their homes.

The trusts that bought these mortgages put them together with thousands of other mortgages. The trusts then divided these pools of mortgages into different sections and sold them to different investors. For example, some investors got rights to be paid from the first payments made by the first 1,000 borrowers, while other investors received only late payments. Some investors would receive no monthly payments but would get the payoffs when borrowers sold or refinanced their homes. These different pieces of the pool were assigned different levels of risk. Because some of these pieces were risky, the trust arranged for insurance to pay the investors if borrowers didn't pay the mortgages.

Remember AIG, which the government bailed out? It was one of the insurance companies that agreed to insure some pieces of these loans. The regulators also failed to regulate the insurance companies for this insurance coverage. When the loans started to go bad, it was clear that AIG wouldn't have enough resources to cover the investors that relied on it for this insurance.

The problem was that some of the investors were pension plans. The investors, including some pension plans, were told by the rating agencies, which are private companies, including Moody's, Standard & Poor's, and Fitch, that these investments were AAA-rated, the highest. However, the rating agencies were paid by the trusts that created these different interests in these pools, so the rating agencies had a big incentive to keep the trusts happy to use them instead of their competitors by giving these different interests high ratings.

The trusts did not "service" these loans; they actually assigned this task to other companies, so the companies to which borrowers made their mortgage payments did not "own" the loans; they got paid just to collect the mortgage payments. These service companies don't have the authority to modify the terms of mortgages and have incentives to just foreclose.

In addition to all this, the trusts wanted to save money in filing fees throughout the country, so they created a company, Mortgage Electronic Registration Systems (MERS). So a mortgage was filed in the name of MERS, but really, MERS just kept track of which trust actually owned any one mortgage. If your mortgage says it's to the benefit of MERS, you must actually ask MERS who the true owner of the mortgage is.

When the electronic age hit and it became very expensive to keep track of original documents, everyone just started scanning documents and getting rid of the originals. In addition, there were many different transfers of these mortgages, and many of them ended up "lost."

While the above is a very simplified version of a very complex story, suffice it to say that there are many different parties involved in any one mortgage. You can't convince an organization servicing your mortgage, an organization that has no financial interest in your mortgage, that it would be better off working with you to restructure your mortgage than to foreclose because it would make more money by foreclosing and thereby collecting additional fees from the investors. Different investors have interests in different parts of your mortgage; what may be a great modification for one investor could be a disaster for another, so the agreements for these pools of mortgages don't allow for modifications.

In addition to this, the system doesn't have the staff it needs to deal with all the foreclosures taking place. What certain mortgage servicing companies did was have employees sign affidavit after affidavit that said that home owners were in default of their mortgages, but those signing had no real way of knowing this for a fact; they were just cranking away, signing legal documents like robots. When this practice became known, the government started investigating the servicers, but the servicers ended up paying fines while the government allowed the foreclosures to go through. Borrowers who had been wrongfully foreclosed on were supposed to be reimbursed, but the government basically put the servicers themselves in charge of deciding which borrowers were wrongfully foreclosed on. Guess what? Essentially, servicers decided that no one had been wrongfully foreclosed on. What a surprise! The government has put into place different mortgage modification programs, including the Making Home Affordable Program (MHA), the Home Affordable Modification Program (HAMP), and the Home Affordable Refinance Program (HARP), and the servicers receive some incentives to agree to modifications to existing mortgages. The servicers, trusts, and investors don't want to make modifications, but they need to make it look as though they're actually doing something. If you're really lucky and have a great financial situation, you might get some help, but only about 3 percent of borrowers actually get any help under these programs because of one overriding fact: those who hold the mortgages cannot be forced to go along with these programs and make modifications; they simply get a little bit of money to entice them to help.

Among the big problems with these programs is that the servicer does not give anyone authority to help the borrower and that the borrowers are required to submit information on a monthly basis, which ends up being too much work for some; many borrowers simply give up in frustration.

The only real hope these borrowers have of actually getting some help is if they get attorneys to hold the servicers accountable in court, but borrowers don't want to spend the money to hire an attorney, and many of them are under the impression they don't need an attorney. This allows the servicers to escape any accountability; they just give borrowers the runaround for several months until the borrowers give up.

Another problem is that people want to avoid bankruptcy and think they can get mortgage modifications by working with the servicers. If borrowers were to file bankruptcy at the beginning of their problems, they could force their servicers to accept a plan to cure arrears, but since they believe they can get a better deal by working with the servicers, they delay considering bankruptcy. When they finally realize they aren't going to get their servicers to help them, they turn to their attorneys and learn that they're tens of thousands of dollars behind and that there's no way they can pay off their arrears over just five years.

When servicers try to foreclose, however, borrowers have some ways of stopping or delaying it. One defense is the simple claim that servicers don't have the right to bring foreclosure actions because they don't own the notes and mortgages. As well, mortgages may be in the name of MERS, but MERS doesn't own anything; it's just a private service that keeps track of who really owns which mortgage. The trust is the entity that needs to bring a foreclosure action.

A second defense is that the original note is gone. Remember, it's expensive and difficult to keep track of originals, so all the parties have are scanned copies. In our court system, we usually require originals to make sure this was what the borrower signed. If the servicer cannot produce the original note, this sometimes stops foreclosure. At other times, the servicer's records are incomplete because the note has been assigned several times to different servicers. The current servicer has no way to verify the information about what the prior servicers did, and sometimes the prior servicers filed bankruptcy and have no one who can testify.

A third defense is that there are no properly recorded documents showing that the party foreclosing was properly assigned the note and mortgage.

A major problem is that the courts don't want to award a borrower a free home, so they really don't like these defenses. However, these tactics can be useful to encourage servicers to sit down and make real deals.

If you want to modify your mortgage, the odd thing is that you must stop making your mortgage payments because the servicer will not talk with you about modifications until your mortgage is in arrears. This obviously puts your home at risk for foreclosure, and the likelihood of success is small, but that likelihood goes up when you have an attorney.

To increase your likelihood of getting a modification, you need to pay your attorney the mortgage payments while you negotiate with the servicer. The attorney will put the money in an escrow account. You have to show you can make the proposed mortgage payments; if you can't, the likelihood of keeping your home is very small.

Finally, our bankruptcy court in Syracuse and Utica has a new program for helping home owners modify their mortgages, and it's a fast-track process. It's under the supervision of the bankruptcy judge, and mortgage loan attorneys have  promised to make these mortgage modifications a priority over other mortgage modification cases. Overall, this program has increased the likelihood of getting mortgage modifications.

Our firm can help home owners seeking mortgage modifications in or out of bankruptcy. There are additional attorneys' fees for this service, but we are seeing a higher likelihood of success in a bankruptcy case because we have more options, including some the lenders are actually required to accept. Also, lenders are happy when borrowers reduce their other debt obligations through bankruptcy.

Tax Repayment Strategies

Tax debts are the most difficult debts to deal with because the government has more methods to collect tax debt than do other creditors. There are different types of tax debt you might encounter. One is real estate property taxes. Real estate property taxes have a first-priority lien on the real property you own. Essentially, I like to think I'm basically "renting" my property from the government because if I don't pay the taxes (the "rent"), the government can foreclose on my interest in the property to collect these taxes. Because property taxes come before the mortgage, most mortgage holders require you pay a certain amount monthly toward the property taxes; they put that in an escrow account and pay the taxes when they come due to make sure they actually get paid. If you get behind in the payment of property taxes, there are three basic strategies to pay them.

One method is to see whether your county will agree to a repayment plan. Generally, counties require large down payments on late taxes and then fairly large periodic payments to catch up while you continue to pay your mortgage. Most of my clients find that the proposals their counties will accept are financially unworkable.

Another method is to file a Chapter 13 bankruptcy; that gives someone who owes taxes five years to pay them off with interest. It's important to put away money to pay for the ongoing property taxes during the Chapter 13 plan period. Generally, this plan works better for most of our clients.

The final method is allowing the mortgage company to pay the taxes as part of a foreclosure or have the county foreclose on the property for back taxes. The county will likely wait until three years of unpaid property taxes have accrued before it forecloses, but this method requires the surrender of the property. As noted above, it takes at least one year for mortgage holders to foreclose in New York, and the average for the last few years has been three years.

Another tax debt clients have is unpaid income tax. Some clients find they owe income taxes because they withdrew IRA or 401k money without adequately holding back enough to pay income taxes on it. Other clients change their tax withholding status at work so they have more money to spend but then end up owing taxes. Some clients owe income taxes because they settled with creditors, but the amount of money the creditors wrote off became income for the debtor in the eyes of the IRS.

Another common complex situation that can come up involves divorced couples disputing who gets to claim the children as deductions. Currently, it appears that the IRS allows the ex who files taxes first to take the deduction regardless of any documents or agreements to the contrary. In business situations, disputes can arise as to whether something is deductible, and problems can arise when one spouse has not been completely honest about the couple's income tax situation and they filed a joint return.

Capital gains taxes can present a problem if the person with the capital gains doesn't have the money to pay them. This can happen when someone buys property for a low price, the property increases in value, and the owner takes out a mortgage on the property based on its increased value. If the owner sells the property, the owner makes money and so owes taxes on the gain but needs all the money to pay off the first mortgage and has none left over to pay taxes on the gain. Some exceptions to this rule for personal homes exist, but these don't apply to other property such as vacation homes.

"Independent contractors," those who are in business for themselves and receive income reported to the IRS on 1099 forms (rather than through paychecks with taxes withheld already) have to pay income taxes quarterly but may not have the money to do so.

It's never a good idea to get yourself in a situation in which you owe taxes you cannot pay. Other debt you might incur is dischargeable in bankruptcy, but taxes basically aren't.

If you plan to dispute claims that you owe taxes, you should get a tax professional to help you fight the IRS. The tax law is extremely complex, and you need a tax-law specialist's expertise. Keep in mind that you will not generally find this level of expertise at your local H&R Block. Such companies may have some specialists, but you'll have to search for them and make sure you're dealing with someone who knows tax laws extremely well. Beware of tax-help companies that advertise on TV; you'll want to deal with someone who can meet face to face with the IRS or other taxing authorities.

If you know you owe the taxes, don't ignore the problem by not filing tax returns or ignoring the notices you get in the mail. If you've done so, find a tax professional who will help you file your taxes correctly as soon as possible and try to negotiate a payment plan. It's always better for you to contact the taxing authorities you owe money to than waiting for them to "find" you.

If you don't dispute that you owe income taxes, your best strategy is to file your taxes on time and ask for a payment plan. If you can't handle the payment plan the IRS offers, let the IRS know that and indicate how much you can afford to pay. If what you're offering is substantially less than what the IRS suggests, you'll need to provide proof of your financial situation. Just because you owe a lot on your credit cards is not a sufficient reason to get a reduction in your payments to the IRS. However, paying child support is more important than paying the IRS.

Sometimes, the IRS will accept the fact that you don't have the financial wherewithal to pay any amount, but again, you must be prepared to show that.

It's important to remain current on your tax payments; if you can't, get in touch with the taxing authorities about the situation. You want to avoid having a tax lien put on you or your property; that's like having a judgment against you, and it could make it impossible for you to get any type of credit. It also has ramifications in a bankruptcy context as well.

Although the bankruptcy code provides for the discharge of income taxes in certain limited situations, the code makes this difficult to nearly impossible, so we cannot guarantee you can successfully discharge taxes. The general rule is that (1) if income (not sales or employee) taxes are over three years old, (2) if tax returns have been filed for two years, and (3) if it's been at least 240 days since the end of an IRS investigation and determination of disputed taxes, it's possible to have your taxes discharged, assuming no fraud or tax warrant/lien.

The three-year rule is calculated based on the date the taxes are due, and if extensions were requested, then the three years start when the extension ended, not when the taxes were filed. For example, 2005 taxes are generally due April 15, 2006. If no extension was requested back then, it may be possible to discharge 2005 taxes after April 15, 2009, assuming other requirements have been met.

If you requested extension until October 15, 2006, and you filed your taxes in July 2006, the earliest you could discharge the taxes would be after October 15, 2009. If the IRS files a tax return for you because you failed to file your taxes, you may not be able to meet the two-year rule under some case law.

If you don't have the money to pay your taxes, file a return and ask for a payment plan. You always want to start the clock ticking on the two-year rule by having filed your tax returns. Once you file your taxes, the IRS may decide to dispute your taxes. If the IRS sends a letter using the term "assessment," you must wait 240 days after the date of this letter to discharge the taxes. For state returns, the assessment starts after the taxes can no longer be appealed.

If fraud is ever involved, the taxes are not dischargeable regardless of the years. Also, if the IRS or other taxing authority claims a tax warrant/lien, the taxes become a secured claim—the taxing authorities have a lien on everything you own, including "exempt" property such as retirement accounts, personal property, and so on. Therefore, even if the tax would have been dischargeable if it were unsecured, the taxes become secured and must be paid with interest to the value of the security. However, they are secured only to the value of your property.

After you file a bankruptcy and receive a discharge, there's no rule that requires the IRS or other taxing authority to tell you that your taxes have been discharged, though sometimes it will send a notice to that effect, and you can also request one. We can write such a request, and we can ask for a determination on the dischargeability of the taxes prior to filing, for a fee. We'll tell you there's a risk that the taxing authorities might get more aggressive in trying to collect (perhaps by imposing a tax warrant) if the taxes are not immediately dischargeable; it can be kind of like waking a sleeping giant.

If you owe taxes and file a Chapter 13 bankruptcy, the taxes must be paid in full during the Chapter 13 plan. At times, the taxes owed exceed what the debtor can afford to pay during the Chapter 13 plan period, but in some cases, we have been able to negotiate with the taxing authorities to permit debtors to remain in Chapter 13; the remaining unpaid taxes will be non-dischargeable and must be paid after the bankruptcy period is over.

Some events will "toll" (or delay) the time periods mentioned above. These events include prior bankruptcies, extensions to file returns, tax litigation, offers in compromise, and requests for collection due-process hearings. Having an installment plan doesn't toll the time periods. If you owe taxes, the best strategy is to set up an installment agreement and pay according to the agreement.

Sales and employment taxes are never dischargeable in bankruptcies; these are usually incurred as part of business operations. If you want to go into business, make sure you understand your responsibilities to the government to avoid digging a hole for yourself that will be nearly impossible to get out of.

If you owe a significant amount in taxes you cannot pay or discharge in bankruptcy, you may want to consider an Offer in Compromise. Trying this with New York State is very difficult because the state doesn't have enough personnel to deal with all the tax problems, and so it relies primarily on computers for its collection process. Be prepared for a frustrating experience getting New York State to consider any proposal, claim, or problem you have with it.

Although you can make an offer by yourself, I'll tell you based on my experience that you're much better off getting the help of an attorney or other tax pro, again avoiding national firms that advertise on TV and the Internet; you need someone willing to meet face to face with any taxing authority. The IRS always treats clients better when they are with attorneys or other tax pros. The IRS has a tendency to throw around certain vocabulary you might not understand, and you might end up failing to provide it with the information and documents it will demand. At that point, IRS personnel will feel justified in mistreating you because you're not coming up with the information they require.

Generally, you must owe a significant amount in taxes to make an Offer in Compromise. For example, if you owe only $5,000, the IRS won't consider an Offer in Compromise. The IRS will require essentially the same information required for filing bankruptcy, so you'll need a detailed report of your income, all your assets, the liens and lien amounts against those assets, and a list of all your liabilities. The IRS and the bankruptcy code use essentially the same budgeting program to determine how much you should be able to pay. The budgeting process and numbers are based on your county and state. The average state income comes into play here, and expenses are based on the county in which you live. If your expenses exceed the average expenses of other households in your county, you'll have to come up with substantiation for your numbers. For example, your medical expenses might be higher because you or a dependent have a serious medical condition, but the IRS will want this to be documented.

Once the IRS has this information about your assets and income, it will figure out how much it could collect if it garnished your wages for ten years. It will add to this the value of all your assets and compare this total to the amount you owe. If it's less than what you owe, the IRS can agree to a compromise that will allow the IRS to get more than this estimated amount. For example, if the amount they could garnish from you in ten years is $10,000, and the net equity in your retirement accounts, car, home, and other property is $5,000, the IRS may accept a compromise for something over $15,000, but be prepared for the IRS to want all that money now.

As you can see from this example, you can't use your own resources to pay that all at once since the IRS is already going to "take" all your equity and projected future income. This is a case in which borrowing from family may make sense because you won't be able to get that money anywhere else. Occasionally, the IRS will accept a payment plan, but it's better not to count on it.

Case History: Daniel Scott

Daniel had a construction business from 2005 to 2008, but some of his projects didn't go well, and he ended up losing money. He gave up his contracting business and started working for a construction company. Rather than paying his IRS debt, he paid his suppliers to prevent them from taking out mechanics' liens on his clients' homes. Although he knew he could not pay the IRS, he filed his tax returns before April 15, 2009.

By July 2010, the IRS assessed his taxes, interest and penalties to be over $20,000. He also owed New York State about $7,000. Daniel makes $25,000/year working, and he collects about $7,500/year in unemployment when he's not working due to weather.

Daniel lost all his assets when the business collapsed; he has an old pickup, no retirement funds, and no real estate. The IRS originally wanted $386/month, and New York State wanted $145/month. Daniel was able to convince the IRS to allow him to pay $125/month, and he got New York State to lower its amount to $50/month. His accountant warned him that those amounts didn't even cover accruing interest, which meant he wouldn't get ahead on his indebtedness.

Daniel and his accountant explored the possibility of an Offer in Compromise, but the accountant realized that neither the IRS nor New York State would agree to reduce the amount owed. The accountant suggested that Daniel make the payments as agreed and try to file a Chapter 7 bankruptcy three years after his tax returns became due in 2009. Daniel struggled, but was able to keep up the payments.

In May 2012, Daniel contacted a bankruptcy attorney. His taxes are dischargeable because they are more than three years old (beyond 4/15/12), they were filed over two years previously (actually he filed them over 3 years ago), and the 240 days since the assessment date of July 2010 had passed. There was no determination or evidence of fraud on Daniel's part. Since Daniel had made the agreed-upon payments to the IRS and New York State, the taxing authorities had not filed tax liens. Finally, these taxes are income taxes and not sales or employee payroll taxes, so they can be discharged in bankruptcy.

Summary of Financial Case:

Single

Wages: $25,000/year

Unemployment: $7,500/ year

Total income: $32,000/year

No tax refunds

No dependents

2001 Ford F-150: paid for; value $2,000

IRS and New York State taxes: $35,000 (because of accrued interest)

No credit cards, medical bills, personal loans, student loans; no child support, no judgments, no cosigners, no gambling losses, no prior bankruptcies.

Since Daniel met all the deadlines for discharging the taxes and since no other viable option is available, it makes sense for him to file bankruptcy at this time. Otherwise, Daniel is looking at trying to pay back the IRS and New York State at a rate that won't let him get ahead of the additional interest he'll be charged. He cannot afford to get a better job or acquire more assets since the IRS and New York State can try to take those assets or demand more money. This is Daniel's best way to get a fresh start.

Documents needed:

- Tax transcripts from the IRS and New York State taxing authorities

- All documents from the taxing authorities, including assessment notices and amount-due notices

- Social Security number and driver's license

- Last two years of tax returns

- Seven months of pay stubs or other records of income

- Title to truck

- Budget

- Credit report

Factors why filing bankruptcy is the best option for Daniel:

First, the amount of debt is significant and growing.

Second, although taxes are normally non-dischargeable, they are dischargeable in this case.

Third, Daniel's income is steady and could increase if he gets a fresh start.

Fourth, his expenses are stable and sufficient for survival.

Fifth, he doesn't have assets that cannot be protected in bankruptcy.

Sixth, the tax debt was due to past events and unlikely to happen again, so Daniel will have a better future after a fresh start.

Daniel had to wait two years from the filing of his tax returns before the taxes could be discharged. If he had wanted to file bankruptcy earlier, we would have recommended that he wait until the taxes could be discharged. If the taxing authorities had filed a tax lien, we might have suggested he file a Chapter 13 and pay to the taxing authorities the value of his limited assets in a Chapter 13 and then 1 percent on the otherwise unsecured portion of the taxing authorities' debt.

Student Loan Repayment Strategies

Our office offers help to student loan borrowers with the following strategies:

1. Helping clients understand their student loan repayments options and create a plan or strategy for repaying or dealing with their student loans.

2. Setting up affordable repayment plans, including help consolidating federal student loans;

3. Assisting clients to qualify for the Public Service Loan Forgiveness program;

4. Helping borrowers get out of default of student loans and stopping administrative wage garnishments, social security offsets, tax refund intercepts and harassing collection calls;

5. Helping disabled borrowers obtain a Total and Permanent Disability Discharge of federal student loans (WARNING! there may be tax consequences for such a discharge);

6. Assisting and/or coaching clients with strategies for repaying, negotiating with or getting sued by private student loan lenders;

7.   Assisting clients, who have suffered violations of the Fair Debt Collection Practices Act by student loan lenders, to obtain damages;

8.   Using Chapter 13 bankruptcy to protect co-signers of private student loans;

9.   Using Chapter 13 bankruptcy to manage federal and private student loan payments;

10.   Bringing "undue" hardship or "non" educational benefit or ineligible school discharge cases in bankruptcy court. (WARNING! These can be expensive and difficult procedures with no guarantee of success. However, we do believe such lawsuits could be the basis for negotiating reasonable repayment plans especially where there is a significant amount in private and federal loans to be repaid.)

The brutal fact is that student loans are today's form of indentured servitude; they're basically non-dischargeable in bankruptcy. Although the bankruptcy code provides for "hardship" discharges in a few circumstances, legal precedents make it nearly impossible to demonstrate "hardship."

Legal cases in which student loan relief was denied include that of a sixty-five-year-old woman working minimum-wage jobs, middle-aged individuals who worked on and off for years at minimum-wage jobs, and single mothers with no work experience trying to support several children. As long as a person is healthy enough to work, judges will never find undue hardship.

It's also expensive to obtain hardship discharges because the courts will require expert witnesses to testify that a person is so disabled that he or she will never work again. If a doctor will agree to write a letter to this effect, it's usually possible to use the informal procedures provided by the student loan creditor to get a discharge without using the bankruptcy system. Many of our clients have accomplished this without an expensive trial and we do assist clients with this process.

There are three types of student loans: federal, state, and private. In the federal loan category are Stafford loans (subsidized and unsubsidized); PLUS loans for parents and graduates; Perkins loans originated by schools; Federal Family Education Loan Program loans (FFELP) (also subsidized and unsubsidized) before July 2010 and originated by banks; and Federal Direct loans (William D. Ford) (subsidized and unsubsidized) and originated by the Department of Education. Each type of student loan has its own options, default rules, and remedy rights. Frankly, the system gets very confusing.

If you have federal student loans, depending on the type of loans, we recommend you attempt to consolidate them and get a consolidated loan repayment plan based on your income (the Income-Based Repayment, or IBR program or Pay As You Earn or PAYE programs are often best). The more you make, the more of your student loan you will pay back; the less you make, the less you will pay. If you're single with a yearly income of less than $25,000, your payment would be $50/month, but if the size of your household is two or more, there's no payment due. We can assist clients with the entire process.

Be aware that under IBR, PAYE and other programs, you might have negative amortization, which means your payments will not be enough to cover the accruing interest, so your student loan balance will increase. However, after twenty-five (and in some cases twenty) years of payments, the balance due will be waived. At that time, you might receive an IRS 1099 form showing the balance that was waived is considered as income on which you'll owe taxes, but this matter hasn't been settled at this time. Be aware that you may be able to consolidate your student loans only once, so make sure you're ready to do so and aren't planning on taking out more.

You can also have your consolidated student loans repaid based on not only income but also on the amount of the loan; this is called the Income-Contingent Repayment (ICR) program, whereas IBR and PAYE is based solely on income. The standard repayment period for student loans is ten years, but IBR, ICR and PAYE repayments can be up to twenty-five years. There are also options for graduated repayments plans; with these, payments start out very low but increase to very high payments.

Consolidation is not available for defaulted private student loans or for loans for which a judgment has been entered. You should not consolidate regular federal loans with Parent Plus loans because it will limit your repayment options.

You should keep in contact with your student loan creditors if you believe you may miss a payment. It's better to try to obtain a deferral than default on your loan because there can be severe penalties for default, including a 25 percent collection fee (you could end up having to pay $2,500 more on a $10,000 loan), and that's in addition to ongoing interest. If you qualify for a deferral with your federal unsubsidized student loans, interest on the student loan principal balance continues to accrue, so you will owe more on your student loan at the end of the deferral, but you'll avoid collection fees. You can get a federal deferral if you're in school more than half time, or if you are unemployed, or if you are deployed in the military or for other hardships.

Federal student loans become delinquent if there has been no payment for less than 270 days, and they are considered in default after 270 days. Upon default, the entire loan becomes due immediately. Those who default on federal student loans can expect to get annoying collection calls, a 15 percent "administrative" (i.e., no lawsuit required) garnishment of wages, an "administrative" interception of tax refunds, a 15 percent garnishment of government benefits such as Social Security, a notation on your credit report of the default, and a Department of Justice lawsuit. You could also be denied FHA or VA home loans if you default on student loans. This could spell disaster for seniors who'll be counting on Social Security.

To cure a default on a federal student loan, you can try to consolidate, but you must act quickly. The feds also have a "rehabilitation" program in which you arrange to pay nine payments in ten months. Once a default has been "cured," the federal government should clear your credit report of the default status. As noted above, we can help clients get out of default and stop the collection efforts.

A few years ago, the government allowed married couples to consolidate their student loans together, but this created a massive problem if they got divorced because there was no way to "unconsolidate" loans. Fortunately, this type of consolidation is no longer available.

If you have a private student loan, the above information is probably not applicable. Private student loans can be more difficult to deal with. First, default occurs the first day you are late with a payment. If the loan goes into default and there is a guarantor, the guarantor's credit report is also notated with the

---

* Much of the information contained in this section came from Joshua Cohen, A student loan lawyer.

default even if the guarantor is ready to make the payments or is unaware of the default.

You cannot consolidate private and federal student loans. Private student loans have a statute of limitations, so private student loan creditors can and will sue you if you default. Also, unlike federal student loans, private student loan creditors can and will go after the guarantor if the person who took out the loan dies; federal student loans, on the other hand, are discharged upon the death of the borrower.

One way to deal with student loans may be to file a Chapter 13 bankruptcy. Chapter 13 payment plans will include student loan obligations. However, in most Chapter 13 plans, the payment going to the student loan creditor will be less than the regular payment and will probably not cover the ongoing interest, and even if you're paying 100 percent to creditors, the student loan payment will probably not cover interest. This means that at the end of the plan, you will still owe money on your student loans and may owe more than you owed prior to starting the plan, depending on the plan payment percentage. Courts have held that you cannot give student loans preferential treatment by paying them a higher percentage than you're paying unsecured creditors. If you need a student loan while you're in a Chapter 13 case, you'll need to get permission from the Chapter 13 trustee.

We've filed Chapter 13 cases in which we reduced the payments for a five-year period, but again, you may owe more than when you started, but at least your cash flow will allow you to survive. We had a client with student loan payments over $1,000/month, which she couldn't afford. We filed a Chapter 13 case and reduced her payments to $125/month.

Be aware that the bankruptcy code says you cannot be denied a student loan because you have filed bankruptcy, but you may need to reapply for a student loan, and this could delay your education. We recommend you be careful about using student loans because they cannot be discharged in bankruptcy, and federal student loans have no statute of limitations, which means they can be collected forever.

It is our experience that if you are delinquent in student loans, the student loan creditor will usually be willing to set up a new payment schedule after the bankruptcy is over. This procedure may be helpful in getting additional student loans to complete your education.

Also, members of the military have unique rights in regards to student loans. This information is detailed in the next chapter, Debt-Management Strategies for Members of the Military.

In summary, student loans are like another tax on your wages for a long time.

Case History: Connie Taylor

Connie is a nurse who works full-time for a nonprofit hospital. She has $48,000 in student loans because she had to support herself and her daughter while she was going through nursing school. After she graduated, she consolidated all her student loans and entered into an IBR. Based on her income and her household size of two, her monthly payments are $350/month. After ten years of making payments, she still owes over $15,500 in student loans. The good news for Connie is that she qualifies for the Public Service Loan Forgiveness (PSLF) program.

Summary of Financial Case:

Single

Income: $44,000/year (average)

Child support: $6,000/year

Tax refunds: $2,500/year

One dependent

2011 Kia Optima: balance $15,000, value $11,000, $375/month payment

No medical, credit card, or personal loan debt.

Student loans: $48,000

No tax debt, no child support, no judgments, no cosigners, no gambling losses, no businesses in the last six years, and no prior bankruptcies.

By using the IBR/Public Service Loan Forgiveness program, Connie can make sure her payments on her student loans are affordable. This gives Connie a lot of flexibility if she needs to reduce her hours to care for her daughter or even take time off if she has additional children and perhaps end up with no payments. This is the fastest way for Connie to pay off her student loans. In addition, loan amounts forgiven under PSLF are not considered income by the IRS. We can help someone like Connie set up this program and help make sure that he or she can qualify for the Loan Forgiveness program.

Documents needed to use this strategy:

- Pay stubs over a ten-year period that prove she worked full-time for a nonprofit or a governmental unit while she made her qualifying student loan payments

- Ten years of qualifying student loan payments (120 such payments, which do not need to be consecutive)

This program is new, it started in 2007, and so it's unknown how exactly it will work; the earliest that PSLF applicants are eligible to apply for forgiveness is October 2017. However, it's best to be prepared and plan carefully. It is possible to work at different governmental or nonprofit institutions and to take breaks in such employment as long as the time worked adds up to ten years. Be aware, however, that some nonprofits may not be eligible for the program, so you should research this before you agree to start a new job.

We are finding that most people with student loans are using strategies that make their situations only worse over the long run. The companies collecting student loans have a huge incentive to grant deferments or provide misinformation about how to find and qualify for the best repayment programs for student loans. Student loan debtors are told they cannot qualify for programs for which they do qualify.

If you owe a significant amount in student loans, it would be to your benefit to get professional help to analyze your situation and help develop a strategy that works best for your situation and then help negotiate with the student loan creditors to make sure they don't give you the wrong information. Only 10 percent of student loan borrowers have taken advantage of the best repayment plan available.

Our office can help those with overwhelming student loan problems develop a plan and strategy for repayment and survival.

Debt-Management Strategies for Members of the Military

Because our nation doesn't want members of its military to be distracted by their debts while they're in harm's way, Congress has enacted laws, including the Soldiers and Sailors Civil Relief Act and the Servicemembers Civil Relief Act to protect them and their families. These provisions apply also to those in the Reserves or the National Guard on active duty. In addition to these provisions, the military provides advice and resources to service members to help them stay out of economic problems or resolve such problems.

Termination of Lease Agreements

Under the law passed by Congress, service members can terminate leases by providing written notice of termination along with orders for active duty as long as the lease was entered into before they started active duty and they or their families occupied the leased premises. The termination date will be the last day of the month after the month in which the notice was given. For example, if notice was given on February 10, termination would be March 30. A landlord cannot withhold security deposits for early termination but may withhold security deposits for damages and for other lawful provisions of the lease agreement.

Since many leases are entered into after a member of the military has started active duty, local military housing offices will work with the service members and landlords to make sure the lease contains a military clause.

Service members can also seek protection from eviction for themselves and their dependents through the courts. If a court finds that the service members' military duties prevent them from paying rent on a timely basis, the judge can order a stay of eviction of up to three months.

Reduced Interest Rates

If members of the military have a hard time paying debts due to their military obligations, they can have the interest rate(s) reduced to 6 percent for the duration of their military commitments. This can apply to credit cards, car loans, and mortgages. Unfortunately, it doesn't apply to federally guaranteed student loans, but it should apply to private student loans.

A service member can request a forbearance, a temporary postponement, of federally guaranteed student loan payments, but interest will continue to accrue. Such debts must be incurred prior to starting active duty; if the debt is incurred after the service member starts active duty, this provision does not apply. Reservist and members of the National Guard routinely use this legal provision.

Lawsuits Stopped/Judgments Avoided

Service members can request a stay, or a postponement, of any legal proceeding in which they're involved. Judgments entered against service members while they're unavailable due to military orders and responsibilities can be voided, and this can apply to civil actions, divorce proceedings, paternity suits, child custody suits, and bankruptcies. This provision does not apply to criminal proceedings, child support determinations, and administrative proceedings, such as those held by military officers to determine fault or wrongdoing. In addition, there's a tolling of the statute of limitations (the time in which actions must be brought) for the period a service member is on active duty, but this doesn't apply to career service members. This tolling will extend the time period that creditors can bring actions against prior service members as well as extend the time service members can file actions against others.

Car Loans and Leases

If car loans or lease agreements are entered into prior to service members' active duty, they can seek protection from repossession unless the creditor gets a court order allowing repossession. Service members must invoke this provision, however, to obtain protection against repossession.

Tax Protections

Service members and their dependents may apply to the court for relief from tax liabilities incurred prior to or during active duty. In addition, courts can grant stays of enforcement so no fines or penalties will accrue.

Student Loans

Soldiers can obtain military deferments of student loans while they are deployed. The military deferment terminates 180 days after the soldier's return from a war, operation or national emergency. Proof, such as military orders or a written statement from a commanding officer, is required to qualify for the military deferment.

In addition, there is a post-active duty deferment which is good for 13 months after active military duty. This post-active deferment runs concurrently (at the same time) as the military deferment if the military deferment is already in place.

Other Assistance

In addition to this legislation, the military has Family Service Centers and Family Ombudsmen to assist service members and their families. These resources offer information about the relocation process and other help, such as help with budgeting, helping a spouse find a new job, parenting classes, and communications skill classes. Furthermore, military chaplains can help members of the military deal with a variety of issues.

The Relocation Assistance Program assists service members and their families who are relocating to other duty stations. They provide welcome kits, assistance with shipping household goods, temporary and long-term housing, financial planning help, child care and medical help, school information, and information about moving overseas among other assistance.

Service members have the right to free legal advice and assistance under the Legal Assistance Program for civil matters. This program is used to help them draft powers of attorney and wills, provide estate planning, review contracts and leases, notarize documents, negotiate with other parties or their attorneys, provide personal financial advice and family relations advice, assist with consumer affairs, provide tax advice, prepare tax returns, deal with landlord-tenant issues, and provide advice on immigration and naturalization issues. This program will at times refer the service members to local civilian attorneys for specialized help or help beyond advice or simple legal drafting work. For additional information, check out: usmilitary.about.com/od/sscra/l/blsscra.html

INFORMATION FOR PROFESSIONALS HELPING OTHERS GET OUT OF DEBT

This section is for ministers, accountants, financial advisors, mortgage brokers, and other professionals who help people get out of debt.

Gathering Information on Assets, Liabilities, and Financial History and Future

When I'm helping people with financial matters and questions, here are the questions I ask:

1. Do you own a home?

   a. What's the amount of your mortgage(s)? How much are your property taxes? Can you show how much you owe on your mortgage(s)? Do you have a copy of a recent real estate property tax bill?

   b. How much could you get for your house at this time?

   c. Is your home jointly owned? Who owes the mortgage? Do you have copies of the recorded deed and mortgage(s)? (The county clerk's office can provide these.)

d. Are you behind in your mortgage(s)? Do you want to keep your home? How much are the monthly payments, including property taxes and insurance?

e. Do you own any other real estate? (Need same info as above.)

2. What year, make, and model are your vehicles? (I use the Kelly Blue Book to come up with values.) Do you have titles to your cars? How much do you owe on them, and how much are you paying per month on them? Are you behind in payments? Do you want to keep your vehicles?

3. What retirement accounts do you have? Are they IRAs, 401ks, or pensions? What percent of your monthly income do you contribute to them? How much is in your checking and savings accounts? Do you have cash hidden under your mattress?

4. Do you have any toys such as four-wheelers or snowmobiles? Do you have valuable tools, jewelry, works of art, stocks, interest in a business, or are you involved in suing someone, or could you pursue a lawsuit against someone? Are you collecting on a personal injury award? In short, what other assets do you own besides your house and vehicles?

5. Other than the house and vehicles, do you have any other secured debt such as a furniture loan? How much are the payments?

6. What do you owe the IRS? The state? For sales or employment taxes? What years are these for?

7. If you owe child support, how much?

8. Do you have any student loans? Are they federal or private loans? Are they cosigned? How much? Current or deferred or defaulted? Type of repayment plan—income based or other? How much are the monthly payments?

9. Has or is someone suing you? Do you have copies of the paperwork?

10. How much do you owe on your credit cards? Personal loans? What are your minimum monthly payments and interest rates on these? How much have you charged in the last six months? How much do you owe in medical bills? (I ask for copies of all bills.)

11. If you owe relatives money, are you paying them back monthly or in periodic lump sums?

12. What are the monthly or yearly incomes for each spouse? Wages, child support payments, unemployment or workers compensation, disability or Social Security income? Any retirement, business, rental, or investment income? Are your income sources steady, seasonal, or variable? (I ask for seven months of pay stubs.)

13. How many people are in your household? Married? Living with someone? How many children live at home? Are you taking care of elderly parents?

14. What's been your financial history? Steady income or periods of unemployment? A student who depends on someone else's income? Have you been sick or disabled? Do you have health insurance?

15. Has there been a divorce or separation? (I ask for a copy of the divorce/separation agreement.) What debts have you agreed to pay as part of the separation?

16. What does your financial future look like? (Same questions as in 14 and 15 above.) How close are you to retiring? Any upcoming changes in household size? Any anticipated needs such as major repairs to home or a new car? Do you have life insurance?

Figuring Out a Budget

The next step in the information-gathering process is coming up with a budget, for which I need:

Wage income–gross; less the following:

Federal taxes

Social Security taxes

Medicare taxes

State taxes

New York State disability

Health insurance

Flex spending for medical expenses

Dental, life, disability, or other insurance

Union dues

Retirement contributions

Retirement loans (total)

Garnishments/support or judgments

Other income, including:

Unemployment

Workers compensation

Retirement income

Business income

Roommate contributions

Relatives' contributions

Rental income

Child/spousal support income

Food stamps, HEAP (Home Energy Assistance Program), and other welfare support

Social Security

Disability income

Tax refunds

Expenses

House payments (including taxes and insurance) or

Rent

Electric and heat (oil, propane, wood?)

Water/sewer

Telephone—cell and landlines

Cable/dish

Online service

Garbage

House maintenance

Food, including cleaning products and diapers

Eating out—lunches, dinners, school lunches

Clothes

Medical expenses—prescriptions, dental costs, eye care costs, etc.

Car payments

Maintenance and gas for car(s)

Entertainment

Charitable contributions

Insurance

    house/renter

    auto

    life

    disability

All credit card and loan payments

Student loan payments

Hair care, pet care, gifts, etc.

Balances of checking and savings accounts (Bank statements will show payments made and income sources.)

This information will put you in a better position to help guide someone to the best options for getting out of debt.

Factors to Consider

While the following six factors must be considered when deciding what method or methods are the best ways to get out of debt, keep in mind that they are all interrelated.

Amount of debt

What is the total amount of debt compared to total yearly income from all sources? If unsecured debt (see number 2 below), especially credit cards, personal loans, and medical bills exceeds $15,000 or is nearly equal to yearly income, bankruptcy must be considered as an option.

Type of debt

If the debt is secured or is non-dischargeable, other options must be considered. If the debt is secured but the person wants to surrender the property, the total debt less the liquidation value of the asset should be considered unsecured. However, if the debt is secured and the person wants to and can afford the payments, this is not a debt that will go away with a bankruptcy. Secured creditors retain their liens even after bankruptcy is filed. Some believe they'll end up with a free car or house if they file bankruptcy, but this isn't the case.

Some debts are not dischargeable in a bankruptcy. These include student loans, child or spousal support, most taxes, criminal restitution, debts incurred by fraud, and debts incurred within three months of filing a bankruptcy. It's important to realize that some debts may be labeled in such a way that they become non-dischargeable. For example, if a party in a separation/ divorce agreement agrees to be responsible for certain debts, those debts are considered non-dischargeable spousal support.

Some debts may be legally dischargeable, but a client may decide to pay them even if they are included in a bankruptcy. Examples could be debts to relatives or medical professionals the debtor wants to continue to use. A bankruptcy discharge of debt doesn't prohibit a debtor from paying off a debt; it just prevents the creditor from trying to collect it, so even if a debtor plans to repay a creditor, bankruptcy may still be the best course of action since it will likely free up income to pay creditors on the debtor's schedule.

Debtors who plan to file bankruptcy should definitely stop incurring any more debt, as it is fraudulent to incur debt after deciding to file bankruptcy. Clients, who go on shopping sprees using their remaining credit just before filing for bankruptcy, will be required to repay these new creditors. Credit card companies will claim fraud if clients transfer balances right before declaring bankruptcy. If the debt is a judgment, it becomes important to file a bankruptcy as soon as possible because a judgment creditor can garnish 10 percent of a debtor's gross income. A judgment creditor can also freeze a debtor's bank account and can use the sheriff's office to uncover information about the debtor and his or her assets and seize those assets. It's better to file a bankruptcy before a judgment is entered because a judgment becomes a judgment lien on real estate owned by the debtor. A bankruptcy alone does not remove the judgment; this requires additional legal proceedings, at an additional cost.

Amount and sources of a debtor's income— steady, variable, short term, long term?

Most often, debt situations arise due to unexpected decreases in income; lately, that's usually the result of job losses, but they can also be due to divorce or separation. Medical conditions may result in lost time at work or even job loss. If the situation is temporary and the person is in a period of transition, trying to get out of debt at that time is probably not a good idea. If the situation looks as though it could become permanent, the person needs to start working to get expenses below income.

Teachers, construction workers, resort workers, and farmers can be subject to seasonal fluctuations in income and should concentrate on saving to handle periods of low or no income. Timing bankruptcies is important in cases such as these because the bankruptcy code looks back at the previous six months only to determine income and assumes that person will make that same amount forever. Bad timing when it comes to filing a bankruptcy could result in a debtor not being able to file a Chapter 7 bankruptcy and instead being forced to file a Chapter 13 bankruptcy and be in bankruptcy, paying creditors for five years.

Amount and source of expenses: Is the expense required for survival? Can the expense be eliminated?

No one will ever get out of debt if he or she can't get expenses below income, so all expenses should be labeled "needs" or "wants." Some may have medical expenses required for survival, and cars are frequently needed to get to and from jobs in Upstate New York and elsewhere.

If debts on items are secured, the debtors still have to determine whether they really need such items. If they're going to file bankruptcy, then it's no big deal to give up secured items. However, if they cannot or will not file bankruptcy, it's important to determine if there will be a deficiency if they give up such items. This is because it may be better to sell such secured items themselves as they will likely get more for them than creditors would by repossession or foreclosure. Selling such items, however, requires the creditors' permission, and the money realized must go to the creditors. This applies to such items as snowmobiles, four-wheelers, furniture, and jewelry. If permission and turnover of proceeds doesn't happen, creditors can possibly repossess the items from the new buyers or have the debtors arrested for conversion of property.

Just because an item is a "want" doesn't mean it must be eliminated from a budget; we all need some diversion or entertainment, and most of my bankruptcy clients "want" cable since it's inexpensive entertainment.

If debtors are behind on mortgage payments, we can use Chapter 13 to catch up those payments. Once debtors file a Chapter 13, they start making regular monthly mortgage payments and pay the arrears over three to five years. This is an effective way to allow debtors to keep their homes while they cure their arrears. If a debtor's second or third mortgages are completely underwater and unsecured, a Chapter 13 could get rid of those mortgages by having them treated as unsecured claims.

Value and type of a debtor's assets (real estate, vehicles, retirement funds, toys such as snowmobiles), liquid assets (such as savings or stock holdings), and claims (such as personal injury judgments

Many assets are protected in bankruptcy, but there are different exemptions under New York and federal law. For example, using New York exemptions, we can protect $82,775 to $165,550 worth of equity (the difference between the full value of the home less the mortgage) in a house depending on whether it's owned by one person or by a husband and wife. We can protect at least $4,425 worth of equity in a vehicle and even more than that if the person doesn't own a home. We can protect most retirement savings. We can protect at least $3,300 in tools of a trade. We can protect at least $5,525 per debtor in household goods. In some cases where there is not homestead exemption (i.e., equity in a home), we can use federal exemptions to protect additional values in other assets.

The matter of exemptions can get very complicated and requires an attorney who understands bankruptcy to determine the correct amounts. Some assets cannot be protected in a bankruptcy, so it's often best to sell them prior to filing bankruptcy. Trustees will likely be more aggressive at going after assets that are more "liquid." To keep trustees from forcing our clients to turn over their liquid assets, we might suggest they sell stock even if it might be exempt in a bankruptcy.

Some assets, such as personal injury judgments, have limited protection in bankruptcy. We might suggest that clients consider waiting to file bankruptcy until after personal injury actions are finalized or consider filing a Chapter 13 bankruptcy so the client can retain control of the lawsuit and the settlement, if any. In a Chapter 7, the trustee can take over a lawsuit and decide on the settlement, which is not likely to be in the client's best interest.

If a debtor has too much equity in a home or other asset, we might suggest filing a Chapter 13 so he or she can retain that asset. In such a case, the debtor must pay creditors over five years what they would have received in a Chapter 7 if the trustee had sold the asset and paid the proceeds to the creditors.

Since most bankruptcy attorneys offer free consultations, you should always have your client check with a bankruptcy attorney to see what, if any, assets wouldn't be protected in a bankruptcy.

Debtor's financial history and future: What caused the debtor to get into debt, and has his or her situation changed for the better or worse?

Most individuals facing severe financial problems have experienced one or more serious setbacks, but the big question is whether the setbacks are temporary or likely to persist for the foreseeable future. If a debtor will need more and expensive medical treatment in the future, a bankruptcy now is probably not the best option; the best time to file a bankruptcy is when things are looking up, cash flow is positive, and medical insurance becomes available for the future.

If a person or a couple's situation is very uncertain for the future and they need the relief bankruptcy can provide, a Chapter 13 might be the best option; it will allow a debtor to dismiss the bankruptcy or may allow the debtor to convert to a Chapter 7 later.

How to find a trusted referral source to help your clients

You want someone with a lot of experience. You want someone who is regulated. You want to find someone who is local, not somewhere across the country. You want someone who understands the applicable federal and state laws. You want someone who makes realistic, believable promises. You want someone recognized as an expert and certified in the field of bankruptcy. You want someone who is receiving updated information and education. You want someone who has written books and articles in this area of expertise. You want someone willing to answer questions. You want someone who will let the person seeking help know if he or she is not the right fit for the services he or she offers. You want someone who cares about your client's long term success.

ABOUT AUTHOR
LAURA COURAGE

Laura Courage finished law school over thirty years ago, graduating third in her class of 127. She started out representing creditors and Chapter 11 debtors in bankruptcy, working for large law firms. As a creditors' attorney, she learned how the other side thinks and works.

Over twenty years ago, Laura started a law firm that represents individuals and couples in Chapter 7 and 13 bankruptcies. She is the only bankruptcy attorney certified by the American Board of Certification in Central New York. Her firm has assisted over 10,000 individuals through the bankruptcy process. Her firm files more bankruptcy cases in the Syracuse and Utica Divisions of the Northern District of New York than any other law firm. Her firm has spent over $150,000 in having the most advanced bankruptcy software available. As a result, her firm has one of the lowest dismissal rates and highest success rates for bankruptcy in the area. Laura, known as The Debtor Doctor ™, loves helping others get out of debt and is passionate about the bankruptcy system.

The following language is required by New York State's Ethical Rules DR 2-105 (C)(1):

"The American Board of Certification is not affiliated with any governmental authority. Certification is not a requirement for the practice of law in the State of New York and does not necessarily indicate greater competence than other attorneys experienced in this field of law."

WA